C-1823   CAREER EXAMINATION SERIES

This is your
PASSBOOK for...

Head Custodian I

Test Preparation Study Guide
Questions & Answers

COPYRIGHT NOTICE

This book is SOLELY intended for, is sold ONLY to, and its use is RESTRICTED to individual, bona fide applicants or candidates who qualify by virtue of having seriously filed applications for appropriate license, certificate, professional and/or promotional advancement, higher school matriculation, scholarship, or other legitimate requirements of education and/or governmental authorities.

This book is NOT intended for use, class instruction, tutoring, training, duplication, copying, reprinting, excerption, or adaptation, etc., by:

1) Other publishers
2) Proprietors and/or Instructors of "Coaching" and/or Preparatory Courses
3) Personnel and/or Training Divisions of commercial, industrial, and governmental organizations
4) Schools, colleges, or universities and/or their departments and staffs, including teachers and other personnel
5) Testing Agencies or Bureaus
6) Study groups which seek by the purchase of a single volume to copy and/or duplicate and/or adapt this material for use by the group as a whole without having purchased individual volumes for each of the members of the group
7) Et al.

Such persons would be in violation of appropriate Federal and State statutes.

PROVISION OF LICENSING AGREEMENTS – Recognized educational, commercial, industrial, and governmental institutions and organizations, and others legitimately engaged in educational pursuits, including training, testing, and measurement activities, may address request for a licensing agreement to the copyright owners, who will determine whether, and under what conditions, including fees and charges, the materials in this book may be used them. In other words, a licensing facility exists for the legitimate use of the material in this book on other than an individual basis. However, it is asseverated and affirmed here that the material in this book CANNOT be used without the receipt of the express permission of such a licensing agreement from the Publishers. Inquiries re licensing should be addressed to the company, attention rights and permissions department.

All rights reserved, including the right of reproduction in whole or in part, in any form or by any means, electronic or mechanical, including photocopying, recording, or by any information storage and retrieval system, without permission in writing from the Publisher.

Copyright © 2024 by
National Learning Corporation

212 Michael Drive, Syosset, NY 11791
(516) 921-8888 • www.passbooks.com
E-mail: info@passbooks.com

PUBLISHED IN THE UNITED STATES OF AMERICA

PASSBOOK® SERIES

THE *PASSBOOK® SERIES* has been created to prepare applicants and candidates for the ultimate academic battlefield – the examination room.

At some time in our lives, each and every one of us may be required to take an examination – for validation, matriculation, admission, qualification, registration, certification, or licensure.

Based on the assumption that every applicant or candidate has met the basic formal educational standards, has taken the required number of courses, and read the necessary texts, the *PASSBOOK® SERIES* furnishes the one special preparation which may assure passing with confidence, instead of failing with insecurity. Examination questions – together with answers – are furnished as the basic vehicle for study so that the mysteries of the examination and its compounding difficulties may be eliminated or diminished by a sure method.

This book is meant to help you pass your examination provided that you qualify and are serious in your objective.

The entire field is reviewed through the huge store of content information which is succinctly presented through a provocative and challenging approach – the question-and-answer method.

A climate of success is established by furnishing the correct answers at the end of each test.

You soon learn to recognize types of questions, forms of questions, and patterns of questioning. You may even begin to anticipate expected outcomes.

You perceive that many questions are repeated or adapted so that you can gain acute insights, which may enable you to score many sure points.

You learn how to confront new questions, or types of questions, and to attack them confidently and work out the correct answers.

You note objectives and emphases, and recognize pitfalls and dangers, so that you may make positive educational adjustments.

Moreover, you are kept fully informed in relation to new concepts, methods, practices, and directions in the field.

You discover that you are actually taking the examination all the time: you are preparing for the examination by "taking" an examination, not by reading extraneous and/or supererogatory textbooks.

In short, this PASSBOOK®, used directedly, should be an important factor in helping you to pass your test.

HEAD CUSTODIAN I

DUTIES:
Supervises all cleaning and maintenance activities in a school building, or a large public library; makes regular inspections of buildings and grounds to maintain proper cleaning and maintenance procedures and makes recommendations for improvements of new equipment; schedules and assigns cleaning and maintenance work of custodians; inspects maintenance work performed by outside contractors; checks to insure that buildings are heated, cleaned, locked and unlocked and in readiness for all activities; reports any acts of vandalism or breakage to proper authorities. Performs related duties as required.

SUBJECT OF EXAMINATION:
The written test designed to evaluate knowledge, skills and /or abilities in the following areas:
1. **Ability to read and follow written instructions** - These questions test for the ability to read, understand and apply written instructions for performing tasks similar to those encountered on the job. All the information needed to answer these questions will be provided in the test booklet.
2. **Building cleaning** - These questions test for knowledge of basic principles and practices of building cleaning. They cover such areas as equipment, tools, supplies, methods and procedures for cleaning different types of surfaces and materials under various, commonly occurring circumstances.
3. **Building operation and maintenance** - These questions test for knowledge of the basic principles, practices and techniques essential to the correct operation and maintenance of public buildings. They cover such areas as building maintenance; preventive maintenance, and minor repair of electrical and plumbing systems; methods and equipment for snow removal; building safety and equipment storage.
4. **Operation and routine maintenance of heating, ventilating and air-conditioning systems** - These questions test for knowledge of basic principles, practices and techniques essential to the correct operation and maintenance of heating, ventilating and air conditioning systems, including such areas as minor cleaning; room temperature and building ventilation control; steam, hot water and hot air heating systems; boiler operation; troubleshooting air conditioning system problems, and proper maintenance of air conditioning systems.
5. **Supervision and training** - These questions test for the knowledge required by a supervisor to set goals, plan and organize work, train workers in how to do their jobs, and direct workers towards meeting established goals. The supervisory questions cover such areas as assigning and reviewing work, evaluating performance, maintaining work quality, motivating employees, increasing efficiency, and dealing with problems that may arise on the job. The training questions cover such areas as determining the necessity for training, selecting appropriate training methods, and evaluating the effectiveness of training.

HOW TO TAKE A TEST

I. YOU MUST PASS AN EXAMINATION

A. *WHAT EVERY CANDIDATE SHOULD KNOW*

Examination applicants often ask us for help in preparing for the written test. What can I study in advance? What kinds of questions will be asked? How will the test be given? How will the papers be graded?

As an applicant for a civil service examination, you may be wondering about some of these things. Our purpose here is to suggest effective methods of advance study and to describe civil service examinations.

Your chances for success on this examination can be increased if you know how to prepare. Those "pre-examination jitters" can be reduced if you know what to expect. You can even experience an adventure in good citizenship if you know why civil service exams are given.

B. *WHY ARE CIVIL SERVICE EXAMINATIONS GIVEN?*

Civil service examinations are important to you in two ways. As a citizen, you want public jobs filled by employees who know how to do their work. As a job seeker, you want a fair chance to compete for that job on an equal footing with other candidates. The best-known means of accomplishing this two-fold goal is the competitive examination.

Exams are widely publicized throughout the nation. They may be administered for jobs in federal, state, city, municipal, town or village governments or agencies.

Any citizen may apply, with some limitations, such as the age or residence of applicants. Your experience and education may be reviewed to see whether you meet the requirements for the particular examination. When these requirements exist, they are reasonable and applied consistently to all applicants. Thus, a competitive examination may cause you some uneasiness now, but it is your privilege and safeguard.

C. *HOW ARE CIVIL SERVICE EXAMS DEVELOPED?*

Examinations are carefully written by trained technicians who are specialists in the field known as "psychological measurement," in consultation with recognized authorities in the field of work that the test will cover. These experts recommend the subject matter areas or skills to be tested; only those knowledges or skills important to your success on the job are included. The most reliable books and source materials available are used as references. Together, the experts and technicians judge the difficulty level of the questions.

Test technicians know how to phrase questions so that the problem is clearly stated. Their ethics do not permit "trick" or "catch" questions. Questions may have been tried out on sample groups, or subjected to statistical analysis, to determine their usefulness.

Written tests are often used in combination with performance tests, ratings of training and experience, and oral interviews. All of these measures combine to form the best-known means of finding the right person for the right job.

II. HOW TO PASS THE WRITTEN TEST

A. NATURE OF THE EXAMINATION

To prepare intelligently for civil service examinations, you should know how they differ from school examinations you have taken. In school you were assigned certain definite pages to read or subjects to cover. The examination questions were quite detailed and usually emphasized memory. Civil service exams, on the other hand, try to discover your present ability to perform the duties of a position, plus your potentiality to learn these duties. In other words, a civil service exam attempts to predict how successful you will be. Questions cover such a broad area that they cannot be as minute and detailed as school exam questions.

In the public service similar kinds of work, or positions, are grouped together in one "class." This process is known as *position-classification*. All the positions in a class are paid according to the salary range for that class. One class title covers all of these positions, and they are all tested by the same examination.

B. FOUR BASIC STEPS

1) Study the announcement

How, then, can you know what subjects to study? Our best answer is: "Learn as much as possible about the class of positions for which you've applied." The exam will test the knowledge, skills and abilities needed to do the work.

Your most valuable source of information about the position you want is the official exam announcement. This announcement lists the training and experience qualifications. Check these standards and apply only if you come reasonably close to meeting them.

The brief description of the position in the examination announcement offers some clues to the subjects which will be tested. Think about the job itself. Review the duties in your mind. Can you perform them, or are there some in which you are rusty? Fill in the blank spots in your preparation.

Many jurisdictions preview the written test in the exam announcement by including a section called "Knowledge and Abilities Required," "Scope of the Examination," or some similar heading. Here you will find out specifically what fields will be tested.

2) Review your own background

Once you learn in general what the position is all about, and what you need to know to do the work, ask yourself which subjects you already know fairly well and which need improvement. You may wonder whether to concentrate on improving your strong areas or on building some background in your fields of weakness. When the announcement has specified "some knowledge" or "considerable knowledge," or has used adjectives like "beginning principles of…" or "advanced … methods," you can get a clue as to the number and difficulty of questions to be asked in any given field. More questions, and hence broader coverage, would be included for those subjects which are more important in the work. Now weigh your strengths and weaknesses against the job requirements and prepare accordingly.

3) Determine the level of the position

Another way to tell how intensively you should prepare is to understand the level of the job for which you are applying. Is it the entering level? In other words, is this the position in which beginners in a field of work are hired? Or is it an intermediate or advanced level? Sometimes this is indicated by such words as "Junior" or "Senior" in the class title. Other jurisdictions use Roman numerals to designate the level – Clerk I, Clerk II, for example. The word "Supervisor" sometimes appears in the title. If the level is not indicated by the title, check the description of duties. Will you be working under very close supervision, or will you have responsibility for independent decisions in this work?

4) Choose appropriate study materials

Now that you know the subjects to be examined and the relative amount of each subject to be covered, you can choose suitable study materials. For beginning level jobs, or even advanced ones, if you have a pronounced weakness in some aspect of your training, read a modern, standard textbook in that field. Be sure it is up to date and has general coverage. Such books are normally available at your library, and the librarian will be glad to help you locate one. For entry-level positions, questions of appropriate difficulty are chosen – neither highly advanced questions, nor those too simple. Such questions require careful thought but not advanced training.

If the position for which you are applying is technical or advanced, you will read more advanced, specialized material. If you are already familiar with the basic principles of your field, elementary textbooks would waste your time. Concentrate on advanced textbooks and technical periodicals. Think through the concepts and review difficult problems in your field.

These are all general sources. You can get more ideas on your own initiative, following these leads. For example, training manuals and publications of the government agency which employs workers in your field can be useful, particularly for technical and professional positions. A letter or visit to the government department involved may result in more specific study suggestions, and certainly will provide you with a more definite idea of the exact nature of the position you are seeking.

III. KINDS OF TESTS

Tests are used for purposes other than measuring knowledge and ability to perform specified duties. For some positions, it is equally important to test ability to make adjustments to new situations or to profit from training. In others, basic mental abilities not dependent on information are essential. Questions which test these things may not appear as pertinent to the duties of the position as those which test for knowledge and information. Yet they are often highly important parts of a fair examination. For very general questions, it is almost impossible to help you direct your study efforts. What we can do is to point out some of the more common of these general abilities needed in public service positions and describe some typical questions.

1) General information

Broad, general information has been found useful for predicting job success in some kinds of work. This is tested in a variety of ways, from vocabulary lists to questions about current events. Basic background in some field of work, such as sociology or economics, may be sampled in a group of questions. Often these are principles which have become familiar to most persons through exposure rather than through formal training. It is difficult to advise you how to study for these questions; being alert to the world around you is our best suggestion.

2) Verbal ability

An example of an ability needed in many positions is verbal or language ability. Verbal ability is, in brief, the ability to use and understand words. Vocabulary and grammar tests are typical measures of this ability. Reading comprehension or paragraph interpretation questions are common in many kinds of civil service tests. You are given a paragraph of written material and asked to find its central meaning.

3) Numerical ability
Number skills can be tested by the familiar arithmetic problem, by checking paired lists of numbers to see which are alike and which are different, or by interpreting charts and graphs. In the latter test, a graph may be printed in the test booklet which you are asked to use as the basis for answering questions.

4) Observation
A popular test for law-enforcement positions is the observation test. A picture is shown to you for several minutes, then taken away. Questions about the picture test your ability to observe both details and larger elements.

5) Following directions
In many positions in the public service, the employee must be able to carry out written instructions dependably and accurately. You may be given a chart with several columns, each column listing a variety of information. The questions require you to carry out directions involving the information given in the chart.

6) Skills and aptitudes
Performance tests effectively measure some manual skills and aptitudes. When the skill is one in which you are trained, such as typing or shorthand, you can practice. These tests are often very much like those given in business school or high school courses. For many of the other skills and aptitudes, however, no short-time preparation can be made. Skills and abilities natural to you or that you have developed throughout your lifetime are being tested.

Many of the general questions just described provide all the data needed to answer the questions and ask you to use your reasoning ability to find the answers. Your best preparation for these tests, as well as for tests of facts and ideas, is to be at your physical and mental best. You, no doubt, have your own methods of getting into an exam-taking mood and keeping "in shape." The next section lists some ideas on this subject.

IV. KINDS OF QUESTIONS

Only rarely is the "essay" question, which you answer in narrative form, used in civil service tests. Civil service tests are usually of the short-answer type. Full instructions for answering these questions will be given to you at the examination. But in case this is your first experience with short-answer questions and separate answer sheets, here is what you need to know:

1) Multiple-choice Questions
Most popular of the short-answer questions is the "multiple choice" or "best answer" question. It can be used, for example, to test for factual knowledge, ability to solve problems or judgment in meeting situations found at work.
A multiple-choice question is normally one of three types—
- It can begin with an incomplete statement followed by several possible endings. You are to find the one ending which *best* completes the statement, although some of the others may not be entirely wrong.
- It can also be a complete statement in the form of a question which is answered by choosing one of the statements listed.

- It can be in the form of a problem – again you select the best answer.

Here is an example of a multiple-choice question with a discussion which should give you some clues as to the method for choosing the right answer:

When an employee has a complaint about his assignment, the action which will *best* help him overcome his difficulty is to
- A. discuss his difficulty with his coworkers
- B. take the problem to the head of the organization
- C. take the problem to the person who gave him the assignment
- D. say nothing to anyone about his complaint

In answering this question, you should study each of the choices to find which is best. Consider choice "A" – Certainly an employee may discuss his complaint with fellow employees, but no change or improvement can result, and the complaint remains unresolved. Choice "B" is a poor choice since the head of the organization probably does not know what assignment you have been given, and taking your problem to him is known as "going over the head" of the supervisor. The supervisor, or person who made the assignment, is the person who can clarify it or correct any injustice. Choice "C" is, therefore, correct. To say nothing, as in choice "D," is unwise. Supervisors have and interest in knowing the problems employees are facing, and the employee is seeking a solution to his problem.

2) True/False Questions

The "true/false" or "right/wrong" form of question is sometimes used. Here a complete statement is given. Your job is to decide whether the statement is right or wrong.

SAMPLE: A roaming cell-phone call to a nearby city costs less than a non-roaming call to a distant city.

This statement is wrong, or false, since roaming calls are more expensive.

This is not a complete list of all possible question forms, although most of the others are variations of these common types. You will always get complete directions for answering questions. Be sure you understand *how* to mark your answers – ask questions until you do.

V. RECORDING YOUR ANSWERS

Computer terminals are used more and more today for many different kinds of exams.

For an examination with very few applicants, you may be told to record your answers in the test booklet itself. Separate answer sheets are much more common. If this separate answer sheet is to be scored by machine – and this is often the case – it is highly important that you mark your answers correctly in order to get credit.

An electronic scoring machine is often used in civil service offices because of the speed with which papers can be scored. Machine-scored answer sheets must be marked with a pencil, which will be given to you. This pencil has a high graphite content which responds to the electronic scoring machine. As a matter of fact, stray dots may register as answers, so do not let your pencil rest on the answer sheet while you are pondering the correct answer. Also, if your pencil lead breaks or is otherwise defective, ask for another.

Since the answer sheet will be dropped in a slot in the scoring machine, be careful not to bend the corners or get the paper crumpled.

The answer sheet normally has five vertical columns of numbers, with 30 numbers to a column. These numbers correspond to the question numbers in your test booklet. After each number, going across the page are four or five pairs of dotted lines. These short dotted lines have small letters or numbers above them. The first two pairs may also have a "T" or "F" above the letters. This indicates that the first two pairs only are to be used if the questions are of the true-false type. If the questions are multiple choice, disregard the "T" and "F" and pay attention only to the small letters or numbers.

Answer your questions in the manner of the sample that follows:

32. The largest city in the United States is
    A. Washington, D.C.
    B. New York City
    C. Chicago
    D. Detroit
    E. San Francisco

1) Choose the answer you think is best. (New York City is the largest, so "B" is correct.)
2) Find the row of dotted lines numbered the same as the question you are answering. (Find row number 32)
3) Find the pair of dotted lines corresponding to the answer. (Find the pair of lines under the mark "B.")
4) Make a solid black mark between the dotted lines.

VI. BEFORE THE TEST

Common sense will help you find procedures to follow to get ready for an examination. Too many of us, however, overlook these sensible measures. Indeed, nervousness and fatigue have been found to be the most serious reasons why applicants fail to do their best on civil service tests. Here is a list of reminders:

- Begin your preparation early – Don't wait until the last minute to go scurrying around for books and materials or to find out what the position is all about.
- Prepare continuously – An hour a night for a week is better than an all-night cram session. This has been definitely established. What is more, a night a week for a month will return better dividends than crowding your study into a shorter period of time.
- Locate the place of the exam – You have been sent a notice telling you when and where to report for the examination. If the location is in a different town or otherwise unfamiliar to you, it would be well to inquire the best route and learn something about the building.
- Relax the night before the test – Allow your mind to rest. Do not study at all that night. Plan some mild recreation or diversion; then go to bed early and get a good night's sleep.
- Get up early enough to make a leisurely trip to the place for the test – This way unforeseen events, traffic snarls, unfamiliar buildings, etc. will not upset you.
- Dress comfortably – A written test is not a fashion show. You will be known by number and not by name, so wear something comfortable.

- Leave excess paraphernalia at home – Shopping bags and odd bundles will get in your way. You need bring only the items mentioned in the official notice you received; usually everything you need is provided. Do not bring reference books to the exam. They will only confuse those last minutes and be taken away from you when in the test room.
- Arrive somewhat ahead of time – If because of transportation schedules you must get there very early, bring a newspaper or magazine to take your mind off yourself while waiting.
- Locate the examination room – When you have found the proper room, you will be directed to the seat or part of the room where you will sit. Sometimes you are given a sheet of instructions to read while you are waiting. Do not fill out any forms until you are told to do so; just read them and be prepared.
- Relax and prepare to listen to the instructions
- If you have any physical problem that may keep you from doing your best, be sure to tell the test administrator. If you are sick or in poor health, you really cannot do your best on the exam. You can come back and take the test some other time.

VII. AT THE TEST

The day of the test is here and you have the test booklet in your hand. The temptation to get going is very strong. Caution! There is more to success than knowing the right answers. You must know how to identify your papers and understand variations in the type of short-answer question used in this particular examination. Follow these suggestions for maximum results from your efforts:

1) Cooperate with the monitor

The test administrator has a duty to create a situation in which you can be as much at ease as possible. He will give instructions, tell you when to begin, check to see that you are marking your answer sheet correctly, and so on. He is not there to guard you, although he will see that your competitors do not take unfair advantage. He wants to help you do your best.

2) Listen to all instructions

Don't jump the gun! Wait until you understand all directions. In most civil service tests you get more time than you need to answer the questions. So don't be in a hurry. Read each word of instructions until you clearly understand the meaning. Study the examples, listen to all announcements and follow directions. Ask questions if you do not understand what to do.

3) Identify your papers

Civil service exams are usually identified by number only. You will be assigned a number; you must not put your name on your test papers. Be sure to copy your number correctly. Since more than one exam may be given, copy your exact examination title.

4) Plan your time

Unless you are told that a test is a "speed" or "rate of work" test, speed itself is usually not important. Time enough to answer all the questions will be provided, but this does not mean that you have all day. An overall time limit has been set. Divide the total time (in minutes) by the number of questions to determine the approximate time you have for each question.

5) Do not linger over difficult questions

If you come across a difficult question, mark it with a paper clip (useful to have along) and come back to it when you have been through the booklet. One caution if you do this – be sure to skip a number on your answer sheet as well. Check often to be sure that you have not lost your place and that you are marking in the row numbered the same as the question you are answering.

6) Read the questions

Be sure you know what the question asks! Many capable people are unsuccessful because they failed to *read* the questions correctly.

7) Answer all questions

Unless you have been instructed that a penalty will be deducted for incorrect answers, it is better to guess than to omit a question.

8) Speed tests

It is often better NOT to guess on speed tests. It has been found that on timed tests people are tempted to spend the last few seconds before time is called in marking answers at random – without even reading them – in the hope of picking up a few extra points. To discourage this practice, the instructions may warn you that your score will be "corrected" for guessing. That is, a penalty will be applied. The incorrect answers will be deducted from the correct ones, or some other penalty formula will be used.

9) Review your answers

If you finish before time is called, go back to the questions you guessed or omitted to give them further thought. Review other answers if you have time.

10) Return your test materials

If you are ready to leave before others have finished or time is called, take ALL your materials to the monitor and leave quietly. Never take any test material with you. The monitor can discover whose papers are not complete, and taking a test booklet may be grounds for disqualification.

VIII. EXAMINATION TECHNIQUES

1) Read the general instructions carefully. These are usually printed on the first page of the exam booklet. As a rule, these instructions refer to the timing of the examination; the fact that you should not start work until the signal and must stop work at a signal, etc. If there are any *special* instructions, such as a choice of questions to be answered, make sure that you note this instruction carefully.

2) When you are ready to start work on the examination, that is as soon as the signal has been given, read the instructions to each question booklet, underline any key words or phrases, such as *least, best, outline, describe* and the like. In this way you will tend to answer as requested rather than discover on reviewing your paper that you *listed without describing*, that you selected the *worst* choice rather than the *best* choice, etc.

3) If the examination is of the objective or multiple-choice type – that is, each question will also give a series of possible answers: A, B, C or D, and you are called upon to select the best answer and write the letter next to that answer on your answer paper – it is advisable to start answering each question in turn. There may be anywhere from 50 to 100 such questions in the three or four hours allotted and you can see how much time would be taken if you read through all the questions before beginning to answer any. Furthermore, if you come across a question or group of questions which you know would be difficult to answer, it would undoubtedly affect your handling of all the other questions.

4) If the examination is of the essay type and contains but a few questions, it is a moot point as to whether you should read all the questions before starting to answer any one. Of course, if you are given a choice – say five out of seven and the like – then it is essential to read all the questions so you can eliminate the two that are most difficult. If, however, you are asked to answer all the questions, there may be danger in trying to answer the easiest one first because you may find that you will spend too much time on it. The best technique is to answer the first question, then proceed to the second, etc.

5) Time your answers. Before the exam begins, write down the time it started, then add the time allowed for the examination and write down the time it must be completed, then divide the time available somewhat as follows:
    - If 3-1/2 hours are allowed, that would be 210 minutes. If you have 80 objective-type questions, that would be an average of 2-1/2 minutes per question. Allow yourself no more than 2 minutes per question, or a total of 160 minutes, which will permit about 50 minutes to review.
    - If for the time allotment of 210 minutes there are 7 essay questions to answer, that would average about 30 minutes a question. Give yourself only 25 minutes per question so that you have about 35 minutes to review.

6) The most important instruction is to *read each question* and make sure you know what is wanted. The second most important instruction is to *time yourself properly* so that you answer every question. The third most important instruction is to *answer every question*. Guess if you have to but include something for each question. Remember that you will receive no credit for a blank and will probably receive some credit if you write something in answer to an essay question. If you guess a letter – say "B" for a multiple-choice question – you may have guessed right. If you leave a blank as an answer to a multiple-choice question, the examiners may respect your feelings but it will not add a point to your score. Some exams may penalize you for wrong answers, so in such cases *only*, you may not want to guess unless you have some basis for your answer.

7) Suggestions
    a. Objective-type questions
        1. Examine the question booklet for proper sequence of pages and questions
        2. Read all instructions carefully
        3. Skip any question which seems too difficult; return to it after all other questions have been answered
        4. Apportion your time properly; do not spend too much time on any single question or group of questions

5. Note and underline key words – *all, most, fewest, least, best, worst, same, opposite,* etc.
6. Pay particular attention to negatives
7. Note unusual option, e.g., unduly long, short, complex, different or similar in content to the body of the question
8. Observe the use of "hedging" words – *probably, may, most likely,* etc.
9. Make sure that your answer is put next to the same number as the question
10. Do not second-guess unless you have good reason to believe the second answer is definitely more correct
11. Cross out original answer if you decide another answer is more accurate; do not erase until you are ready to hand your paper in
12. Answer all questions; guess unless instructed otherwise
13. Leave time for review

b. Essay questions
   1. Read each question carefully
   2. Determine exactly what is wanted. Underline key words or phrases.
   3. Decide on outline or paragraph answer
   4. Include many different points and elements unless asked to develop any one or two points or elements
   5. Show impartiality by giving pros and cons unless directed to select one side only
   6. Make and write down any assumptions you find necessary to answer the questions
   7. Watch your English, grammar, punctuation and choice of words
   8. Time your answers; don't crowd material

8) Answering the essay question

Most essay questions can be answered by framing the specific response around several key words or ideas. Here are a few such key words or ideas:

M's: manpower, materials, methods, money, management
P's: purpose, program, policy, plan, procedure, practice, problems, pitfalls, personnel, public relations

   a. Six basic steps in handling problems:
      1. Preliminary plan and background development
      2. Collect information, data and facts
      3. Analyze and interpret information, data and facts
      4. Analyze and develop solutions as well as make recommendations
      5. Prepare report and sell recommendations
      6. Install recommendations and follow up effectiveness

   b. Pitfalls to avoid
      1. *Taking things for granted* – A statement of the situation does not necessarily imply that each of the elements is necessarily true; for example, a complaint may be invalid and biased so that all that can be taken for granted is that a complaint has been registered

2. *Considering only one side of a situation* – Wherever possible, indicate several alternatives and then point out the reasons you selected the best one
3. *Failing to indicate follow up* – Whenever your answer indicates action on your part, make certain that you will take proper follow-up action to see how successful your recommendations, procedures or actions turn out to be
4. *Taking too long in answering any single question* – Remember to time your answers properly

IX. AFTER THE TEST

Scoring procedures differ in detail among civil service jurisdictions although the general principles are the same. Whether the papers are hand-scored or graded by machine we have described, they are nearly always graded by number. That is, the person who marks the paper knows only the number – never the name – of the applicant. Not until all the papers have been graded will they be matched with names. If other tests, such as training and experience or oral interview ratings have been given, scores will be combined. Different parts of the examination usually have different weights. For example, the written test might count 60 percent of the final grade, and a rating of training and experience 40 percent. In many jurisdictions, veterans will have a certain number of points added to their grades.

After the final grade has been determined, the names are placed in grade order and an eligible list is established. There are various methods for resolving ties between those who get the same final grade – probably the most common is to place first the name of the person whose application was received first. Job offers are made from the eligible list in the order the names appear on it. You will be notified of your grade and your rank as soon as all these computations have been made. This will be done as rapidly as possible.

People who are found to meet the requirements in the announcement are called "eligibles." Their names are put on a list of eligible candidates. An eligible's chances of getting a job depend on how high he stands on this list and how fast agencies are filling jobs from the list.

When a job is to be filled from a list of eligibles, the agency asks for the names of people on the list of eligibles for that job. When the civil service commission receives this request, it sends to the agency the names of the three people highest on this list. Or, if the job to be filled has specialized requirements, the office sends the agency the names of the top three persons who meet these requirements from the general list.

The appointing officer makes a choice from among the three people whose names were sent to him. If the selected person accepts the appointment, the names of the others are put back on the list to be considered for future openings.

That is the rule in hiring from all kinds of eligible lists, whether they are for typist, carpenter, chemist, or something else. For every vacancy, the appointing officer has his choice of any one of the top three eligibles on the list. This explains why the person whose name is on top of the list sometimes does not get an appointment when some of the persons lower on the list do. If the appointing officer chooses the second or third eligible, the No. 1 eligible does not get a job at once, but stays on the list until he is appointed or the list is terminated.

X. HOW TO PASS THE INTERVIEW TEST

The examination for which you applied requires an oral interview test. You have already taken the written test and you are now being called for the interview test – the final part of the formal examination.

You may think that it is not possible to prepare for an interview test and that there are no procedures to follow during an interview. Our purpose is to point out some things you can do in advance that will help you and some good rules to follow and pitfalls to avoid while you are being interviewed.

What is an interview supposed to test?

The written examination is designed to test the technical knowledge and competence of the candidate; the oral is designed to evaluate intangible qualities, not readily measured otherwise, and to establish a list showing the relative fitness of each candidate – as measured against his competitors – for the position sought. Scoring is not on the basis of "right" and "wrong," but on a sliding scale of values ranging from "not passable" to "outstanding." As a matter of fact, it is possible to achieve a relatively low score without a single "incorrect" answer because of evident weakness in the qualities being measured.

Occasionally, an examination may consist entirely of an oral test – either an individual or a group oral. In such cases, information is sought concerning the technical knowledges and abilities of the candidate, since there has been no written examination for this purpose. More commonly, however, an oral test is used to supplement a written examination.

Who conducts interviews?

The composition of oral boards varies among different jurisdictions. In nearly all, a representative of the personnel department serves as chairman. One of the members of the board may be a representative of the department in which the candidate would work. In some cases, "outside experts" are used, and, frequently, a businessman or some other representative of the general public is asked to serve. Labor and management or other special groups may be represented. The aim is to secure the services of experts in the appropriate field.

However the board is composed, it is a good idea (and not at all improper or unethical) to ascertain in advance of the interview who the members are and what groups they represent. When you are introduced to them, you will have some idea of their backgrounds and interests, and at least you will not stutter and stammer over their names.

What should be done before the interview?

While knowledge about the board members is useful and takes some of the surprise element out of the interview, there is other preparation which is more substantive. It *is* possible to prepare for an oral interview – in several ways:

1) Keep a copy of your application and review it carefully before the interview

This may be the only document before the oral board, and the starting point of the interview. Know what education and experience you have listed there, and the sequence and dates of all of it. Sometimes the board will ask you to review the highlights of your experience for them; you should not have to hem and haw doing it.

2) Study the class specification and the examination announcement

Usually, the oral board has one or both of these to guide them. The qualities, characteristics or knowledges required by the position sought are stated in these documents. They offer valuable clues as to the nature of the oral interview. For example, if the job involves supervisory responsibilities, the announcement will usually indicate that knowledge of modern supervisory methods and the qualifications of the candidate as a supervisor will be tested. If so, you can expect such questions, frequently in the form of a hypothetical situation which you are expected to solve. NEVER go into an oral without knowledge of the duties and responsibilities of the job you seek.

3) Think through each qualification required

Try to visualize the kind of questions you would ask if you were a board member. How well could you answer them? Try especially to appraise your own knowledge and background in each area, *measured against the job sought*, and identify any areas in which you are weak. Be critical and realistic – do not flatter yourself.

4) Do some general reading in areas in which you feel you may be weak

For example, if the job involves supervision and your past experience has NOT, some general reading in supervisory methods and practices, particularly in the field of human relations, might be useful. Do NOT study agency procedures or detailed manuals. The oral board will be testing your understanding and capacity, not your memory.

5) Get a good night's sleep and watch your general health and mental attitude

You will want a clear head at the interview. Take care of a cold or any other minor ailment, and of course, no hangovers.

What should be done on the day of the interview?

Now comes the day of the interview itself. Give yourself plenty of time to get there. Plan to arrive somewhat ahead of the scheduled time, particularly if your appointment is in the fore part of the day. If a previous candidate fails to appear, the board might be ready for you a bit early. By early afternoon an oral board is almost invariably behind schedule if there are many candidates, and you may have to wait. Take along a book or magazine to read, or your application to review, but leave any extraneous material in the waiting room when you go in for your interview. In any event, relax and compose yourself.

The matter of dress is important. The board is forming impressions about you – from your experience, your manners, your attitude, and your appearance. Give your personal appearance careful attention. Dress your best, but not your flashiest. Choose conservative, appropriate clothing, and be sure it is immaculate. This is a business interview, and your appearance should indicate that you regard it as such. Besides, being well groomed and properly dressed will help boost your confidence.

Sooner or later, someone will call your name and escort you into the interview room. *This is it.* From here on you are on your own. It is too late for any more preparation. But remember, you asked for this opportunity to prove your fitness, and you are here because your request was granted.

What happens when you go in?

The usual sequence of events will be as follows: The clerk (who is often the board stenographer) will introduce you to the chairman of the oral board, who will introduce you to the other members of the board. Acknowledge the introductions before you sit down. Do not be surprised if you find a microphone facing you or a stenotypist sitting by. Oral interviews are usually recorded in the event of an appeal or other review.

Usually the chairman of the board will open the interview by reviewing the highlights of your education and work experience from your application – primarily for the benefit of the other members of the board, as well as to get the material into the record. Do not interrupt or comment unless there is an error or significant misinterpretation; if that is the case, do not hesitate. But do not quibble about insignificant matters. Also, he will usually ask you some question about your education, experience or your present job – partly to get you to start talking and to establish the interviewing "rapport." He may start the actual questioning, or turn it over to one of the other members. Frequently, each member undertakes the questioning on a particular area, one in which he is perhaps most competent, so you can expect each member to participate in the examination. Because time is limited, you may also expect some rather abrupt switches in the direction the questioning takes, so do not be upset by it. Normally, a board member will not pursue a single line of questioning unless he discovers a particular strength or weakness.

After each member has participated, the chairman will usually ask whether any member has any further questions, then will ask you if you have anything you wish to add. Unless you are expecting this question, it may floor you. Worse, it may start you off on an extended, extemporaneous speech. The board is not usually seeking more information. The question is principally to offer you a last opportunity to present further qualifications or to indicate that you have nothing to add. So, if you feel that a significant qualification or characteristic has been overlooked, it is proper to point it out in a sentence or so. Do not compliment the board on the thoroughness of their examination – they have been sketchy, and you know it. If you wish, merely say, "No thank you, I have nothing further to add." This is a point where you can "talk yourself out" of a good impression or fail to present an important bit of information. Remember, *you close the interview yourself.*

The chairman will then say, "That is all, Mr. _____, thank you." Do not be startled; the interview is over, and quicker than you think. Thank him, gather your belongings and take your leave. Save your sigh of relief for the other side of the door.

How to put your best foot forward

Throughout this entire process, you may feel that the board individually and collectively is trying to pierce your defenses, seek out your hidden weaknesses and embarrass and confuse you. Actually, this is not true. They are obliged to make an appraisal of your qualifications for the job you are seeking, and they want to see you in your best light. Remember, they must interview all candidates and a non-cooperative candidate may become a failure in spite of their best efforts to bring out his qualifications. Here are 15 suggestions that will help you:

1) Be natural – Keep your attitude confident, not cocky

If you are not confident that you can do the job, do not expect the board to be. Do not apologize for your weaknesses, try to bring out your strong points. The board is interested in a positive, not negative, presentation. Cockiness will antagonize any board member and make him wonder if you are covering up a weakness by a false show of strength.

2) Get comfortable, but don't lounge or sprawl

Sit erectly but not stiffly. A careless posture may lead the board to conclude that you are careless in other things, or at least that you are not impressed by the importance of the occasion. Either conclusion is natural, even if incorrect. Do not fuss with your clothing, a pencil or an ashtray. Your hands may occasionally be useful to emphasize a point; do not let them become a point of distraction.

3) Do not wisecrack or make small talk

This is a serious situation, and your attitude should show that you consider it as such. Further, the time of the board is limited – they do not want to waste it, and neither should you.

4) Do not exaggerate your experience or abilities

In the first place, from information in the application or other interviews and sources, the board may know more about you than you think. Secondly, you probably will not get away with it. An experienced board is rather adept at spotting such a situation, so do not take the chance.

5) If you know a board member, do not make a point of it, yet do not hide it

Certainly you are not fooling him, and probably not the other members of the board. Do not try to take advantage of your acquaintanceship – it will probably do you little good.

6) Do not dominate the interview

Let the board do that. They will give you the clues – do not assume that you have to do all the talking. Realize that the board has a number of questions to ask you, and do not try to take up all the interview time by showing off your extensive knowledge of the answer to the first one.

7) Be attentive

You only have 20 minutes or so, and you should keep your attention at its sharpest throughout. When a member is addressing a problem or question to you, give him your undivided attention. Address your reply principally to him, but do not exclude the other board members.

8) Do not interrupt

A board member may be stating a problem for you to analyze. He will ask you a question when the time comes. Let him state the problem, and wait for the question.

9) Make sure you understand the question

Do not try to answer until you are sure what the question is. If it is not clear, restate it in your own words or ask the board member to clarify it for you. However, do not haggle about minor elements.

10) Reply promptly but not hastily

A common entry on oral board rating sheets is "candidate responded readily," or "candidate hesitated in replies." Respond as promptly and quickly as you can, but do not jump to a hasty, ill-considered answer.

11) Do not be peremptory in your answers

A brief answer is proper – but do not fire your answer back. That is a losing game from your point of view. The board member can probably ask questions much faster than you can answer them.

12) Do not try to create the answer you think the board member wants

He is interested in what kind of mind you have and how it works – not in playing games. Furthermore, he can usually spot this practice and will actually grade you down on it.

13) Do not switch sides in your reply merely to agree with a board member

Frequently, a member will take a contrary position merely to draw you out and to see if you are willing and able to defend your point of view. Do not start a debate, yet do not surrender a good position. If a position is worth taking, it is worth defending.

14) Do not be afraid to admit an error in judgment if you are shown to be wrong
   The board knows that you are forced to reply without any opportunity for careful consideration. Your answer may be demonstrably wrong. If so, admit it and get on with the interview.

15) Do not dwell at length on your present job
   The opening question may relate to your present assignment. Answer the question but do not go into an extended discussion. You are being examined for a *new* job, not your present one. As a matter of fact, try to phrase ALL your answers in terms of the job for which you are being examined.

Basis of Rating
   Probably you will forget most of these "do's" and "don'ts" when you walk into the oral interview room. Even remembering them all will not ensure you a passing grade. Perhaps you did not have the qualifications in the first place. But remembering them will help you to put your best foot forward, without treading on the toes of the board members.
   Rumor and popular opinion to the contrary notwithstanding, an oral board wants you to make the best appearance possible. They know you are under pressure – but they also want to see how you respond to it as a guide to what your reaction would be under the pressures of the job you seek. They will be influenced by the degree of poise you display, the personal traits you show and the manner in which you respond.

ABOUT THIS BOOK

   This book contains tests divided into Examination Sections. Go through each test, answering every question in the margin. We have also attached a sample answer sheet at the back of the book that can be removed and used. At the end of each test look at the answer key and check your answers. On the ones you got wrong, look at the right answer choice and learn. Do not fill in the answers first. Do not memorize the questions and answers, but understand the answer and principles involved. On your test, the questions will likely be different from the samples. Questions are changed and new ones added. If you understand these past questions you should have success with any changes that arise. Tests may consist of several types of questions. We have additional books on each subject should more study be advisable or necessary for you. Finally, the more you study, the better prepared you will be. This book is intended to be the last thing you study before you walk into the examination room. Prior study of relevant texts is also recommended. NLC publishes some of these in our Fundamental Series. Knowledge and good sense are important factors in passing your exam. Good luck also helps. So now study this Passbook, absorb the material contained within and take that knowledge into the examination. Then do your best to pass that exam.

EXAMINATION SECTION

EXAMINATION SECTION
TEST 1

DIRECTIONS: Each question or incomplete statement is followed by several suggested answers or completions. Select the one that BEST answers the question or completes the statement. *PRINT THE LETTER OF THE CORRECT ANSWER IN THE SPACE AT THE RIGHT.*

1. The KEY figure in any custodial safety program is the
   A. custodian   B. cleaner   C. mayor   D. commissioner

2. A custodian must inspect or have a maintenance man inspect every window cleaner's safety belt AT LEAST
   A. each time the windows are washed
   B. once a month
   C. once a year
   D. once every second year

3. A custodian's written instruction to his staff on the subject of security in public buildings should include instructions to
   A. exclude the public at all times
   B. admit the public at all times
   C. admit the public only if they are neat and well-dressed
   D. admit the public during specified hours

4. A custodian in charge of a building who is normally on duty during the daytime hours in a building which is cleaned at night should
   A. never make night inspections since he is not responsible for the cleanliness of the building
   B. make night inspections at least once a year
   C. never make night inspections because the cleaners will think he is spying on them
   D. make night inspections at least twice a month

5. The employee MOST likely to find the nests and runways in a building of roaches and vermin is a
   A. maintenance man   B. building custodian
   C. night cleaner   D. stationary fireman

6. When mopping, the pails containing the cleaning solutions should be
   A. slid along the floor to avoid injury due to lifting
   B. kept off the floor, preferably on a rolling platform
   C. shifted from place to place using a mop
   D. equipped with a spigot for applying the mopping solution

7. Of the following, the item that is considered a concrete floor sealer is
   A. water wax
   B. sodium hypochlorite
   C. sodium silicate
   D. linseed oil

   7._____

8. A material COMMONLY used in detergent is
   A. rock salt
   B. Glauber's salt
   C. tri-sodium phosphate
   D. monosodium glutamate

   8._____

9. A disinfectant material is one that will
   A. kill germs
   B. dissolve soil and stop odors
   C. give a clean odor and cover a disagreeable odor
   D. prevent soil buildup

   9._____

10. When scrubbing a wooden floor, it is ADVISABLE to
    A. flood the surface with the cleaning solution in order to float the soil out of all crevices
    B. hose off the loosened soil before starting the scrubbing operation
    C. pick up the used solution as soon as possible
    D. mix a mild acid with the cleaning solution in order to clean the surface quickly

    10._____

11. Before starting a wall washing operation, it is BEST to
    A. check the temperature of the water
    B. soak the sponge to be used
    C. check the pH of the mixed cleaning solution
    D. dust the wall to be washed

    11._____

12. Of the following, the MOST nearly correct statement regarding the economical operation of the heating system in a building is that
    A. the heat should always be shut down at 4 P.M. and turned on at 8 A.M.
    B. the heat should be shut down only over the weekend
    C. it is best to keep the heat on at all times so that the number of complaints are kept to a minimum
    D. the times at which the heat is shut down and turned on should be varied depending on the prevailing outdoor temperature

    12._____

13. A floor made of marble or granite chis imbedded in cement is USUALLY called
    A. terrazzo   B. linoleum   C. palmetto   D. parquet

    13._____

14. In a 4-wire, 3-phase electrical supply system, the voltage between one phase and ground used for the lighting is MOST NEARLY
    A. 440   B. 230   C. 208   D. 115

    14._____

15. Of the following, the one that takes the place of a fuse in an electrical circuit is a
    A. transformer
    B. circuit breaker
    C. condenser
    D. knife switch

    15._____

16. Gas bills are USUALLY computed on the basis of
    A. cubic feet   B. gallons   C. pounds   D. kilowatts

17. An operating oil-fired steam boiler explosion may sometimes be caused by
    A. carrying too high a water level in the boiler
    B. inadequate purging of combustion chamber between fires
    C. overfiring the boiler
    D. carrying too high an oil temperature

18. The one of the following commercial sizes of anthracite which is the LARGEST in size is
    A. stove   B. chestnut   C. pea   D. rice

19. Assume that six windows of a public building facing one street have been consistently broken by boys playing ball after hours and over weekends.
    The BEST solution to this problem is to
    A. post a no ball playing sign on the wall
    B. erect protective screening outside the six windows
    C. post a guard on weekend patrol duty
    D. request special weekend police protection for the property

20. The BEST method or tool to use for cleaning dust from an unplastered cinder-block wall is
    A. a Tampico brush with stock cleaning solution
    B. a vacuum cleaner
    C. water under pressure from hose and nozzle
    D. a feather duster

21. Of the following, the LARGEST individual item of expense in operating a public building is generally the cost of
    A. cleaning   B. heating fuel
    C. electricity   D. elevator service

22. The CHIEF purpose for changing the handle of a floor brush from one side of the brush block to the other side is to
    A. allow the janitor to change hands
    B. make both sides of the brush equally dirty
    C. give both sides of the brush equal wear
    D. change the angle of sweeping

23. Of the following, the weight of mop MOST likely used in the nightly mopping of corridors, halls, or lobbies is _____ ounce.
    A. 8   B. 16   C. 24   D. 50

24. After sweeping assignment is completed, floor brushes should be stored
    A. in a pan of water
    B. by hanging the brushes on pegs or nails
    C. by piling the brushes on each other carefully
    D. in a normal sweeping position, bristles resting on the floor

25. Nylon-treated scrubbing discs
    A. require more water than scrubbing brushes
    B. require more detergent solution than scrubbing brushes
    C. must be used with cold water only
    D. are generally more effective than steel wool pads

26. Of the following, the BEST material to use to clean exterior bronze is
    A. pumice   B. paste wax
    C. wire wheel on portable buffer   D. lemon oil polish

27. The use of trisodium phosphate in cleaning polished marble should be AVOIDED because it
    A. may cause spalling
    B. discolors the surface of the marble
    C. builds up a slick surface on the marble
    D. pits the glazed surface and bleaches the marble

28. The floor area, in square feet, on which a properly treated dustless sweeping cloth can be used before the cloth must be washed is
    A. 500-1000   B. 2000-3000   C. 4000-6000   D. 8000-10000

29. A cleaning woman working a six-hour shift should be able to cover (clean) _____ Gilbert work units.
    A. 100-200   B. 400-500   C. 1100-1200   D. 6000-7000

30. An incipient fire is one which
    A. has just started and can be readily extinguished using an ordinary hand extinguisher
    B. occurs only in motor vehicles
    C. is burning out of control in a storeroom
    D. is a banked coal fire

31. Maintaining room temperature at 75°F in the winter time will increase fuel consumption above the amount needed to maintain 70°F by APPROXIMATELY
    A. 5%   B. 10%   C. 15%   D. 20%

32. Of the following, the one which represents the BEST practical combustion condition in an oil-fired low pressure steam plant is _____ stack temperature.
    A. 8% CO_2 - 500°F   B. 13% CO_2 - 400°F
    C. 10% CO_2 - 700°F   D. 6% CO_2 - 400°F

33. An office has floor dimensions of 6 ft. 6 in. wide by 22 ft. 0 in. long. The floor area of this office, in square feet, is MOST NEARLY
    A. 143   B. 263   C. 363   D. 463

34. Dollies are USUALLY used
    A. as convenient platforms upon which to store items
    B. as ornamental protective covers

C. to raise items to the required level
D. to transport items from one place to another

35. When lifting a heavy object from a table, which of the following rules is it MOST important to observe?
    A. Do not bend your knees.
    B. Do not stand too close to the object.
    C. Keep your back straight.
    D. Keep your shoulder level with the object

36. The FIRST objective of all fire prevention is
    A. confining fire to a limited area
    B. safeguarding life against fire
    C. reducing insurance rates
    D. preventing property damage

37. A custodian should know the equipment used in his work well enough to
    A. make any repairs which might be needed
    B. know what parts to remove in case of breakdown
    C. anticipate any reasonable possibility of a breakdown
    D. know all the lubricants specified by the manufacturer

38. The PRIMARY responsibility of a supervising custodian is to
    A. make friends of all subordinates
    B. search for new methods of doing the work
    C. win the respect of his superior
    D. get the work done properly within a reasonable time

39. When a custodian believes that the work of a subordinate is below standard, he should
    A. assign the employee to work that is considered undesirable
    B. do nothing immediately in the hope that the employee will bring his work up to standard without any help from the supervisor
    C. reduce the privileges of the employee at once
    D. discuss it as soon as possible with the employee

40. An office worker frequently complains to the custodian that her office is poorly illuminated.
    The BEST action for the custodian to follow is to
    A. ignore the complaints as those of an habitual crank
    B. inform the worker that illumination is a fixed item built into the building originally and evidently is the result of faulty planning by the architect
    C. request a licensed electrician to install additional ceiling lights
    D. investigate for faulty illumination features in the room, such as dirty lamp globes and incorrect lamp wattages

KEY (CORRECT ANSWERS)

1.	A	11.	D	21.	A	31.	D
2.	C	12.	D	22.	C	32.	B
3.	D	13.	A	23.	C	33.	C
4.	D	14.	D	24.	B	34.	D
5.	B	15.	B	25.	D	35.	C
6.	B	16.	A	26.	D	36.	B
7.	C	17.	B	27.	A	37.	C
8.	C	18.	A	28.	C	38.	D
9.	A	19.	B	29.	C	39.	D
10.	C	20.	B	30.	A	40.	D

TEST 2

DIRECTIONS: Each question or incomplete statement is followed by several suggested answers or completions. Select the one that BEST answers the question or completes the statement. *PRINT THE LETTER OF THE CORRECT ANSWER IN THE SPACE AT THE RIGHT.*

1. Of the following, the MOST important reason for the custodian to plan work schedules for men under his supervision is that
    A. emergency situations can easily be handled if they should arise
    B. it insures that essential operations will be adequately covered
    C. the men will be more satisfied if a routine is established
    D. the relationship between the supervisor and his subordinate will be clarified

    1._____

2. Sealers for open-grained wood floors should NOT contain linseed oil because
    A. the linseed oil would damage the wood fibers
    B. the linseed oil would deteriorate mop strands
    C. water wax would penetrate the linseed oil sealer and rot the wood
    D. linseed oil on wood take too long to dry satisfactorily before a floor finish could be applied

    2._____

3. When washing painted wall areas by hand, a man should be expected to wash each hour an area, in square feet, equal to
    A. 75-125   B. 150-300   C. 400-600   D. 750-1000

    3._____

4. Of the following, the one that is MOST desirable to use in dusting furniture is a
    A. feather duster   B. paper towel
    C. counter brush   D. soft cotton cloth

    4._____

5. The one of the following floor types on which oily sweeping compound may be used is
    A. vinyl tile   B. concrete   C. linoleum   D. terrazzo

    5._____

6. A steam heating system where the steam and condensate flow in the same pipe is called a _____ system.
    A. one pipe gravity return   B. sub-atmospheric
    C. vacuum return   D. zone control

    6._____

7. A test of a boiler by applying pressure equal to or greater than the maximum working pressure is called a _____ test.
    A. hydrostatic   B. barometric   C. hygroscopic   D. gyroscopic

    7._____

8. A stack switch, as used with an oil burner,
    A. shuts down the burner in case of non-ignition
    B. shuts down the burner in case of high stack temperatures
    C. controls the flow of secondary air
    D. operates the barometric damper

    8._____

7

9. The vertical pipes leading from the steam mains to the radiators are called
   A. drip lines
   B. risers
   C. radiant coils
   D. expansion joints

10. Fuel oil storage tanks are equipped with vents.
    The purpose of these vents is to
    A. make tank soundings
    B. check oil flash points
    C. fill the fuel tanks
    D. allow air to mix

11. A compound gauge in a boiler room
    A. measures steam and water pressure
    B. shows the quantity of boiler treatment compound on hand
    C. measures pressures above and below atmospheric pressure
    D. indicates the degree of compounding in a steam engine

12. Of the following, the CHIEF purpose of insulating steam lines is to
    A. prevent loss of heat
    B. protect people from being burned by them
    C. prevent leaks
    D. protect the pipes against corrosion

13. The MOST important function of thermostatic traps on radiators is to
    A. regulate the heat given off by the radiators
    B. remove water and air from the radiator
    C. assist the steam pressure in filling the radiator
    D. maintain a vacuum within the radiator

14. The designation *1/8-27N.P.T.* USUALLY indicates
    A. machine screw thread
    B. pipe thread
    C. spur gear size
    D. sprocket chain size

15. The size of a chisel is determined by its
    A. length   B. width   C. pitch   D. height

16. The cause of paint blisters is USUALLY
    A. moisture under the paint coat
    B. too thick a coat of paint
    C. too much oil in paint
    D. the plaster pores not sealed properly

17. A wood-framed picture is to be attached to a plaster and hollow tile wall.
    Of the following, the PROPER installation would include the use of
    A. wire cut nails
    B. miracle glue
    C. expansion shields and screws
    D. self-tapping screws

3 (#2)

18. The PROPER tool or method to use for driving a finish nail to the depth necessary for puttying when installing wood trim is
    A. countersink
    B. another nail of the same diameter
    C. a nail set
    D. a center punch

    18.____

19. Faucet leakage in a large building is BEST controlled by periodic
    A. faucet replacement
    B. addition of a sealing compound to the water supply
    C. packing replacement
    D. faucet inspection and repair

    19.____

20. Escutcheons are USUALLY located
    A. on kitchen cabinet drawers
    B. on windows
    C. around pipes, to cover pipe sleeve openings
    D. around armored electric cable going into a gem box

    20.____

21. It is ADVISABLE to remove broken bulbs from light sockets with
    A. a wooden or hard rubber wedge
    B. pliers
    C. a hammer and chisel
    D. a fuse puller

    21.____

22. A room 20' x 25' in area with a ceiling height of 9'6" is to be painted. One gallon of paint will cover 400 square feet.
    The MINIMUM number of gallons necessary to give the four walls and the ceiling one coat of paint is
    A. 2   B. 3   C. 4   D. 5

    22.____

23. Of the following, the ones on which gaskets are MOST likely to be used are
    A threaded pipe plugs   B. cast iron pipe nipples
    C. flanged pipe fittings   D. threaded cast iron reducing tees

    23.____

24. If a 110 volt lamp were used on a 220 volt circuit, the
    A. fuse would burn out   B. lamp would burn out
    C. line would overheat   D. lamp would flicker

    24.____

25. The third prong on the plug of portable electric power tools of recent manufacture is for
    A. using the tool on a 3-phase power outlet
    B. eliminating interference in radio or television sets
    C. grounding the tool as a safety precaution
    D. using the tool on direct current circuits

    25.____

26. When changing brushes on a scrubbing machine, of the following, the FIRST step to take is to
    A. lock the switch in the *off* position
    B. be sure the power cable electric plug supplying the machine is disconnected from the wall outlet
    C. place the machine on top of the positioned brushes
    D. dip the brushes in water

26.____

27. In cleaning away branches that have been broken off as a result of a severe storm, one of your men comes in contact with a live electric line and falls unconscious.
    After having removed him from contact, the FIRST thing to be done is to
    A. send for an inhalator to revive him
    B. administer mouth-to-mouth resuscitation
    C. search for the switch to prevent any other such cases
    D. loosen his clothing and begin rubbing his forehead to restore circulation

27.____

28. Of the following, the MOST effective way to reduce waste in cleaning equipment and tools is by
    A. requiring a worn brush or broom to be returned before issuing a new one
    B. requiring the cleaners to use all cleaning tools for specific periods of time
    C. keeping careful records of how frequently cleaning equipment and tools are issued to cleaners
    D. making sure that cleaners use the tools properly

28.____

29. A window cleaner should carefully examine his safety belt
    A. once a week
    B. before he puts it on each time
    C. once a month
    D. once before he enters a building

29.____

30. One of your cleaners was injured as a result of slipping on an oily floor.
    This type of accident is MOST likely due to
    A. defective equipment
    B. the physical condition of the cleaner
    C. failure to use proper safety appliances
    D. poor housekeeping

30.____

31. One important use of accident reports is to provide information that may be used to reduce the possibility of similar accidents.
    The MOST valuable entry on the report for this purpose is the
    A. name of the victim
    B. injury sustained by the victim
    C. cause of the accident
    D. location of the accident

31.____

32. Fires in buildings are of such complexity that
    A. no plans or methods of attack can be formulated in advance
    B. no planned procedures can be relied on
    C. an appointed committee is necessary to direct fighting at the fire
    D. the problem must be considered in advance and methods of attack formulated

32.____

33. Of the following types of fires, a soda-acid fire extinguisher is NOT recommended for
    A. electric motor controls
    B. waste paper
    C. waste rags
    D. wood desks

34. A foam-type fire extinguisher extinguishes fires by
    A. cooling only
    B. drenching only
    C. smothering only
    D. cooling and smothering

35. If a keg of nails had on it the words *Net Weight 10 pounds*, it would mean that the
    A. keg weighed 10 pounds without the nails
    B. nails and the keg together weighed 10 pounds
    C. nails weighed 10 pounds without the keg
    D. weight of 10 pounds is approximate

36. In deciding which items should be stored together, the one of the following factors which is usually of LEAST importance is
    A. activity   B. class   C. cost   D. size

37. Of the following, the MOST effective way to teach a subordinate how to store an item is to
    A. do it yourself while explaining
    B. explain the procedure verbally
    C. have him do it while you criticize
    D. let him look at photographs of the operation

38. If a cleaner is doing excellent work, then the PROPER action of the custodian is to
    A. give him preferential assignments as a reward
    B. tell the other cleaners what excellent work he is doing
    C. praise his work at the earlies opportunity
    D. do nothing since the man may become over-confident

39. A cleaner does very good work, but he has trouble getting to work on time. To get the man to come on time, you should
    A. bring him up on charges to stop the lateness once and for all
    B. have him report directly to you every time he is late
    C. talk over the problem with him to find its cause and possible solution
    D. threaten to transfer him if he cannot get to work on time

40. When the National flag is to be flown at half staff, it should ALWAYS be hoisted
    A. slowly to half staff
    B. slowly to the peak of staff and then lowered slowly to half staff
    C. briskly to the peak of staff and then lowered slowly to half staff
    D. briskly to the peak of staff and then lowered briskly to half staff

KEY (CORRECT ANSWERS)

1.	B	11.	C	21.	A	31.	C
2.	D	12.	A	22.	C	32.	D
3.	B	13.	B	23.	C	33.	A
4.	D	14.	B	24.	B	34.	D
5.	B	15.	B	25.	C	35.	C
6.	A	16.		26.	B	36.	C
7.	A	17.	C	27.	B	37.	A
8.	A	18.	C	28.	D	38.	C
9.	B	19.	C	29.	B	39.	C
10.	D	20.	D	30.	D	40.	C

EXAMINATION SECTION
TEST 1

DIRECTIONS: Each question or incomplete statement is followed by several suggested answers or completions. Select the one that BEST answers the question or completes the statement. *PRINT THE LETTER OF THE CORRECT ANSWER IN THE SPACE AT THE RIGHT.*

1. There are a considerable number of forms and reports to be submitted on schedule by a building custodian.
   The ADVISABLE method of accomplishing this duty is to

   A. fill out the reports at odd times during the days when you have free time
   B. schedule a definite period of the work week for completing these forms and reports
   C. assign your foreman or cleaner to handle all these forms for you and to have them available on time
   D. classify or group the forms and reports and fill out only one of each group and refer the other forms or reports to the ones completed

1.____

2. In enforcing compliance with safety regulations, you should take the attitude that they must be complied with because

   A. every accident can be prevented
   B. safety regulations are based on reason and experience with the best methods of accident prevention
   C. compliance with safety regulations will make other safety efforts unnecessary
   D. they are the law, and law enforcement is an end in itself

2.____

3. The use of trisodium phosphate in cleaning marble should be avoided because

   A. it discolors the surface of the marble
   B. the salt crystals get in the pores, expand, and crack the marble
   C. it pits the glazed surface and bleaches the marble
   D. it builds up a slick surface on the marble

3.____

4. The use of a concentrated cleaning solution on painted or varnished woodwork

   A. results in burning the pigments of paint or varnish, causing dull, streaky surfaces
   B. cuts down on time and energy in maintaining clean, unblemished surfaces
   C. insures spotless, clean, bright surfaces
   D. is detrimental to the health of the cleaners

4.____

5. A building custodian will make the BEST impression on the office staff if he

   A. impresses them with the importance of his job
   B. says little and is cold and distant
   C. is easy-going and good-natured
   D. is courteous and performs his duties with as little delay as possible

5.____

6. Domestic hot water storage reservoirs should be thoroughly cleaned once

   A. a week   B. a month
   C. a year   D. every two years

6.____

7. A *pH* value of 4 would indicate a(n)　　　　　　　　　　　　　　　　　　　　　　　　　　　7._____

   A. acid solution
   B. neutral solution
   C. alkaline solution
   D. low pressure heating system

8. When the diaphragm or bellows of a thermostatic radiator trap is found to be dirty, it is　　8._____
   USUALLY cleaned with

   A. turpentine
   B. carbon tetrachloride
   C. kerosene
   D. mild soap and water

9. The CHIEF purpose of a plumbing trap is to　　　　　　　　　　　　　　　　　　　　　　　9._____

   A. permit air to enter the sewer
   B. prevent the entrance of sewer gas into the building
   C. break the shock of the water draining off
   D. siphon off the waste water

10. The safety device on the gas pilot flame of a gas-fired apparatus should operate on pilot　10._____
    flame failure to

    A. bypass the main gas supply directly to the flue
    B. switch over to auxiliary bottled gas pilot flame
    C. shut off the gas supply
    D. introduce sufficient excess air to keep the furnace below the lower explosive limit

11. When instructing employees in regard to their duties in case of fire, a supervisor should　11._____

    A. tell employees to take no action until the fire department equipment has arrived
    B. tell all employees to go to the scene of the fire
    C. assign each employee specific duties
    D. tell employees to extinguish the fire before calling the supervisor or the fire department

12. The PRINCIPAL value of a good report is that it　　　　　　　　　　　　　　　　　　　　　12._____

    A. is always available for reference
    B. impresses department heads with the need for immediate action
    C. reflects upon the writer of the report
    D. expedites official business

13. The quality of work performed by personnel engaged in building cleaning is BEST evaluated by　13._____

    A. studying building cleaning expenditures
    B. studying time records of personnel
    C. analyzing complaints by building occupants
    D. inspecting the building periodically

14. Of the following, a building custodian need NOT be kept informed on　　　　　　　　　　　14._____

    A. departmental management policies
    B. terms of union contracts covering his subordinates
    C. developments of current interest in custodial operations
    D. current rate of interest on municipal bonds

15. The BEST way to make work assignments to persons required to clean a multi-story building is to

   A. allow the persons to pick their room or area assignments out of a hat
   B. make specific room or area assignments to each person separately
   C. rotate room and area assignments daily according to a chart posted on the bulletin board
   D. each week let a different member of the group make the room or area assignment

16. One important use of accident reports is to provide information that may be used to reduce the possibility of similar accidents.
The MOST valuable entry on the report for this purpose is the

   A. name of the victim
   B. injury sustained by the victim
   C. cause of the accident
   D. location of the accident

17. Suppose that an emergency has arisen which requires you to cancel some of the jobs scheduled for that day.
Of the following jobs, the one that can be eliminated for that day with LEAST effect on the proper operation and maintenance of the building is

   A. mopping and cleaning toilet rooms
   B. checking public stairs and corridors for hazards
   C. improving the location of supplies in the storeroom
   D. replacing broken window panes in offices

18. Of the following, a building custodian's attitude toward grievances should be to

   A. pay little attention to little grievances
   B. be very alert to grievances and make adjustments in existing conditions to appease all of them
   C. know the most frequent causes of grievances and strive to prevent them from arising
   D. maintain rigid discipline of a nature that *smoothes out* all grievances

19. A heavy snowfall must be removed from the sidewalks around the building. You, as building custodian, have assigned two men to shovel snow from the walks. After an interval, you check and find they are bickering as to how much each is shoveling, and no snow is being removed.
In this situation, you should

   A. stand with them to supervise the snow removal and to be sure the work is divided evenly
   B. assign two other men to snow removal and send the original two back to their usual chores
   C. put the man with seniority in full charge of the other man
   D. separate the men by sending them to opposite ends of the walks to shovel alone, with a warning that you will be checking on their progress at short intervals

20. Of the following, safety on the job is BEST assured by 20.____

    A. keeping alert
    B. following every rule
    C. working very slowly
    D. never working alone

KEY (CORRECT ANSWERS)

1.	B	11.	C
2.	B	12.	D
3.	B	13.	D
4.	A	14.	D
5.	D	15.	B
6.	C	16.	C
7.	A	17.	C
8.	C	18.	C
9.	B	19.	D
10.	C	20.	A

TEST 2

DIRECTIONS: Each question or incomplete statement is followed by several suggested answers or completions. Select the one that BEST answers the question or completes the statement. *PRINT THE LETTER OF THE CORRECT ANSWER IN THE SPACE AT THE RIGHT.*

1. A foam-type fire extinguisher extinguishes fires by 1.____

   A. cooling *only*
   B. drenching *only*
   C. smothering *only*
   D. cooling and smothering

2. The extinguishing agent in a soda-acid fire extinguisher is 2.____

   A. carbon dioxide
   B. water
   C. carbon tetrachloride
   D. calcium chloride solution

3. The PROPER extinguisher to use on an electrical fire in an operating electric motor is 3.____

   A. foam
   B. carbon dioxide
   C. soda and acid
   D. water

4. When an extension ladder is in place and ready to be used, the rope used to extend the ladder should be 4.____

   A. left hanging free out of the way of the climber's feet
   B. used to raise and lower tools to the man on the ladder
   C. used as a means of steadying the climber
   D. tied securely around a lower rung

5. The PRINCIPAL characteristic of panic locks or bolts on doors of places of public assembly is that they 5.____

   A. allow the doors to open outwardly with sufficient pressure on the bars of the lock
   B. allow the doors to open inwardly with sufficient pressure on the bars of the lock
   C. prevent the door from opening under impact load
   D. may be opened with any tumbler lock key

6. The MAIN purpose of periodic inspections and tests of electrical equipment is to 6.____

   A. encourage the men to take better care of the equipment
   B. make the men familiar with the equipment
   C. discover minor faults before they develop into major faults
   D. keep the men busy during otherwise slack periods

7. Standard, extra strong, and double extra strong welded steel pipe of a given size all have the SAME 7.____

   A. outside diameter
   B. inside diameter
   C. average diameter
   D. flow capacity for any given flow velocity

8. In reference to domestic gas piping,

   A. couplings with running threads are used to join pipes
   B. risers must have a drip leg and cap at bottom
   C. gasketed unions may be used in joining pipe
   D. composition disc globe valves are used to throttle the gas

9. Chewing gum should be removed from rubber, asphalt, or linoleum flooring with

   A. a putty knife   B. steel wool
   C. gritty compounds   D. a solvent

10. Which one of the following is the BEST procedure to follow when the linoleum floor of a meeting room containing movable furniture is to be mopped?

    A. The furniture should be moved by sliding it along the floor to prevent injury to the cleaners.
    B. The furniture should not be moved.
    C. The furniture should be moved by lifting it and carrying it to a clear spot to prevent damage to the linoleum.
    D. Very little water should be used in order to prevent the legs of the furniture from getting wet.

11. Asphalt tile flooring that has been subjected to oily compounds

    A. may last indefinitely
    B. must be removed and replaced with new asphalt tile immediately
    C. may be restored to hardness and lustre by several moppings with hot water and several applications of water wax
    D. must be restored to original condition by several moppings with kerosene

12. The use of alcohol in water for washing windows is NOT recommended because it

    A. is a hazard to the cleaner in that he may be affected by the fumes
    B. will damage the paint around the edges of the glass
    C. pits the surface of the glass
    D. destroys the bristles of the brush applying the solution to the pane

13. Of the following, the BEST material to use for removing grass stains on marble or wood is

    A. oxalic acid   B. chloride of lime
    C. sodium silicate   D. sodium hypochlorite

14. Shades or Venetian blinds are PREFERABLY cleaned with a

    A. feather duster   B. counter brush
    C. damp sponge   D. vacuum cleaner

15. Asphalt tile floors are PREFERABLY polished with

    A. water emulsion wax   B. wax in solution with benzol
    C. a high fatty acid soap   D. sodium metaphosphate

16. Washing soda is used to 16._____

    A. eliminate the need for rinse mopping or wiping
    B. make the cleaning compound abrasive
    C. decrease the wetting power of water
    D. increase the wetting power of water

17. Varnish or lacquer may be used as a sealer on floors finished with 17._____

    A. asphalt tiles
    B. linoleum
    C. rubber tiles
    D. cork tiles

18. A long-handled deck scrub brush is MOST effective when scrubbing 18._____

    A. large open areas
    B. stair treads
    C. small flat areas
    D. long corridors

19. The BEST method for preventing the infestation of a building by rats is to 19._____

    A. use cats
    B. use rat traps
    C. eliminate rat harborages in the building
    D. use poisoned bait

20. The one of the following foodstuffs which, if allowed to remain on ordinary asphalt tile, will MOST likely be most injurious to it is 20._____

    A. milk
    B. maple syrup
    C. ketchup
    D. salad oil

KEY (CORRECT ANSWERS)

1.	D	11.	C
2.	B	12.	B
3.	B	13.	D
4.	D	14.	D
5.	A	15.	A
6.	C	16.	D
7.	A	17.	D
8.	B	18.	C
9.	A	19.	C
10.	C	20.	D

TEST 3

DIRECTIONS: Each question or incomplete statement is followed by several suggested answers or completions. Select the one that BEST answers the question or completes the statement. *PRINT THE LETTER OF THE CORRECT ANSWER IN THE SPACE AT THE RIGHT.*

1. Employees engaged in cleaning operations who are issued rubber gloves to protect their hands against caustic solutions should be warned that 1.____

   A. such solution allowed to spill over the glove top into the space between the glove and the hand may damage the skin of the hand
   B. rubber gloves have a very short life in contact with caustic solutions
   C. harmful gases can penetrate the rubber and harm even dry hands
   D. contact of the hands with glove-type rubber for over an hour is harmful

2. Pyrethrins are used as 2.____

   A. insecticides   B. germicides
   C. waxes   D. detergents

3. Water hammer is 3.____

   A. a special hammer used to remove scale from a radiator
   B. caused by water in steam lines
   C. caused by excessive boiler pressure
   D. caused by low water level in the boiler

4. Which of the following is USUALLY used in the construction of a steam pressure gauge? 4.____

   A. Perfect circle tube   B. Venturi tube
   C. Bourdon tube   D. Elastic linkage

5. Usually when a large room is gradually filled with people, the room temperature 5.____

   A. and humidity both decrease
   B. increases and the humidity decreases
   C. and humidity increase
   D. decreases and humidity increases

6. A foot valve at the intake end of the suction line of a pump serves MAINLY to 6.____

   A. maintain pump prime
   B. filter out large particles in the fluid
   C. increase the maximum suction lift of the pump
   D. increase pump flow rate

7. A pressure gauge attached to a standpipe system shows a pressure of 36 pounds per sq. in. 7.____
   The head of water, in feet, above the gauge is MOST NEARLY

   A. 24   B. 36   C. 60   D. 83

8. Of the following, the term *vapor barrier* would MOST likely be associated with

   A. electric service installation
   B. insulation materials
   C. fuel oil tank installation
   D. domestic gas piping

9. Pitot tubes are used to

   A. test feed water for impurities
   B. measure air or gas flow in a duct
   C. prevent overheating of elements of a steam gauge
   D. control the ignition system of an oil burner

10. In warm air heating and in ventilating systems, laboratories and kitchens should NOT be equipped with return ducts in order to

    A. keep air velocities in other returns as high as possible
    B. reduce fire hazards
    C. reduce the possibility of circulating odors through the system
    D. keep the temperature high in these rooms

11. One square foot of equivalent direct steam radiation (EDR) is equivalent to a heat emission of _____ BTU per _____.

    A. 150; hour
    B. 240; minute
    C. 150; minute
    D. 240; hour

12. Of the following, the one which is LEAST likely to cause continuous vibration of an operating motor is

    A. a faulty starting circuit
    B. excessive belt tension
    C. the misalignment of motor and driven equipment
    D. loose bearings

13. The function of a steam trap is to

    A. remove sediment and dirt from steam
    B. remove air and non-condensible gases from steam
    C. relieve excessive steam pressure to the atmosphere
    D. remove condensate from a pipe or an apparatus

14. The temperature at which air is just saturated with the moisture present in it is called its

    A. relative humidity
    B. absolute humidity
    C. humid temperature
    D. dew point

15. If scale forms on the seat of a float-operated boiler feed water regulator, the MOST likely result is

    A. internal corrosion of the boiler shell
    B. insufficient supply of water to the boiler
    C. flooding of the boiler
    D. shutting down of the oil burner by the low water cut-out

16. The compound gauge in the oil suction line shows a high vacuum. This is USUALLY an indication of

    A. a dirty oil strainer
    B. low oil level in the fuel oil storage tank
    C. a leak in the fuel oil preheater
    D. an obstruction in the fuel oil preheater

17. Of the following, the information which is LEAST important on a boiler room log sheet is the

    A. stack temperature readings
    B. CO_2 readings
    C. number of boilers in operation
    D. boiler room humidity

18. Pitting and corrosion of the water side of the boiler heating surfaces is due MAINLY to the boiler water containing dissolved

    A. oxygen
    B. hydrogen
    C. soda-ash
    D. sodium sulphite

19. The combustion efficiency of a boiler can be determined with a CO_2

    A. flue gas temperature
    B. boiler room humidity
    C. outside air temperature
    D. under fire draft

20. The try-cocks of steam boilers are used to

    A. find the height of water in the boiler
    B. test steam pressure in the boiler
    C. empty the boiler of water
    D. act as safety valves

KEY (CORRECT ANSWERS)

1.	A	11.	D
2.	A	12.	A
3.	B	13.	D
4.	C	14.	D
5.	C	15.	C
6.	A	16.	A
7.	D	17.	D
8.	B	18.	A
9.	B	19.	A
10.	C	20.	A

TEST 4

DIRECTIONS: Each question or incomplete statement is followed by several suggested answers or completions. Select the one that BEST answers the question or completes the statement. *PRINT THE LETTER OF THE CORRECT ANSWER IN THE SPACE AT THE RIGHT.*

1. The reason for sweating inside a refrigerator cabinet is   1.____

    A. high percent running time of compressor unit
    B. high cabinet air temperature
    C. defective expansion valve
    D. a poor door seal

2. Of the following ingredients, the ones to be mixed with water to *point-up* the brickwork of a building are: 1 part cement,   2.____

    A. 2 parts sand, 3 parts gravel
    B. 3 parts sand, 4 parts gravel
    C. 3 parts sand
    D. 5 parts sand

3. Acid soils can BEST be neutralized by liberal applications of   3.____

    A. manure   B. salt
    C. lime   D. powdered-basalt

4. Summer blooming flower bulbs should be stored in a _____ place.   4.____

    A. warm, dry   B. warm, moist
    C. cool, moist   D. cool, dry

5. A certain 31-day month had an average temperature of 45 Fahrenheit. The number of degree days for this month is   5.____

    A. 31   B. 450   C. 620   D. 1395

6. While concrete is *curing*, it is MOST desirable to   6.____

    A. expose the concrete to sun and air as much as possible
    B. keep the concrete surface moist
    C. maintain a temperature of not more than 60°F
    D. maintain a temperature of at least 80°F

7. To join two lengths of pipe together in a solid straight run, the fitting to use is a   7.____

    A. coupling   B. tee
    C. hickey   D. shoulder nipple

8. New copper flashing that has been soldered should be   8.____

    A. muriatic acid   B. plain water
    C. benzine   D. washing soda or lye

9. The intercooler of a two-stage air compressor is connected to the compressor between the

   A. two stages
   B. filter and the first stage
   C. second stage and the receiver
   D. receiver and point of usage of the air

10. Both terms *tank* and *close* apply USUALLY to

    A. electric generator couplings
    B. freon storage units
    C. pipe nipples
    D. ventilation plenum chambers

11. The commercial fertilizer *5-10-5* refers to

    A. 5% nitrogen, 10% phosphoric acid, 5% potash
    B. 5% rotted manure, 10% calcium chloride, 5% bone meal
    C. 5% soda, 10% tobacco dust, 5% bone meal
    D. 5% tobacco dust, 10% rotted manure, 5% sulphur

12. The slope or slant of a soil line is 1/4" per foot. If this drainage line is 50' long, the difference in elevation from one end to the other is, in feet, MOST NEARLY

    A. 0.55   B. 1.04   C. 2.08   D. 12.5

13. Oil is used with sharpening stones when sharpening wood chisels in order to

    A. reduce the effort needed to move the blade over the stone
    B. maintain the oil temper of the steel used for the chisel
    C. flush off the small metal chips and clear the cutting edges of the abrasive grit
    D. reduce the temperature due to friction

14. A maintenance man checking a refrigerator for a freon leak would use a

    A. soap and water solution
    B. halide torch
    C. glycerine solution
    D. linseed oil and whiting solution

15. A basement floor area of 5000 square feet is under 9 inches of water.
    If this 9 inches of water is to be pumped out of the basement in one hour, the required capacity of the portable pump, in gallons per minute, is MOST NEARLY

    A. 63   B. 470   C. 1020   D. 2810

16. A MAJOR advantage of keeping a perpetual inventory of supplies is that it

    A. gives a current record of the supplies available at all times
    B. reduces the work required to distribute supplies
    C. avoids the need for periodic physical inventories
    D. shows who is using excessive supplies

17. Employees generally do NOT object to strict rules and regulations if they

   A. are enforced without bias or favor
   B. result in more material gain
   C. deal with relatively unimportant phases of the work
   D. affect the supervisors more than their subordinates

18. In order to have building employees willing to follow standardized cleaning and maintenance procedures, the supervisor MUST be prepared to

   A. work alongside the employees
   B. demonstrate the reasonableness of the procedures
   C. offer incentive pay for their use
   D. be adamant in opposing changes in the standardized procedures

19. Of the following, the MOST important step when accepting incoming shipments of standard items normally carried in stock is to check the items for

   A. electrical performance
   B. chemical composition
   C. quantity delivered
   D. mechanical performance

20. The orderly arrangement of supplies in storage USUALLY

   A. takes too much time to be worthwhile
   B. is important only in large warehouses
   C. is essential for stock selection and inventory purposes
   D. cannot be accomplished when package sizes vary

KEY (CORRECT ANSWERS)

1.	D	11.	A
2.	C	12.	B
3.	C	13.	C
4.	D	14.	B
5.	C	15.	B
6.	B	16.	A
7.	A	17.	A
8.	D	18.	B
9.	A	19.	C
10.	C	20.	C

EXAMINATION SECTION
TEST 1

DIRECTIONS: Each question or incomplete statement is followed by several suggested answers or completions. Select the one that BEST answers the question or completes the statement. *PRINT THE LETTER OF THE CORRECT ANSWER IN THE SPACE AT THE RIGHT.*

1. Of the following, the PREFERRED sequence of tasks to be followed in office cleaning is 1.____

   A. dust desks, empty ash trays and waste baskets, mop floor
   B. mop floor, dust desks, empty ash trays and waste baskets
   C. empty ash trays and waste baskets, dust desks, mop floor
   D. mop floor, empty ash trays and waste baskets, dust desks

2. When vacuum cleaning rugs, the suction tool should be pushed 2.____

   A. diagonally across the lay of the nap
   B. with the lay of the nap
   C. across the lay of the nap
   D. against the lay of the nap

3. The brownish discoloration that sometimes occurs in hot water circulating systems is USUALLY due to 3.____

   A. molds   B. algae   C. bacteria   D. rust

4. The type of valve that does NOT have a stuffing or packing gland is a _____ valve. 4.____

   A. globe   B. radiator   C. check   D. gate

5. Assuming that the hot and cold water demand of a fixture will be the same, then the normal size of the hot water pipe with respect to that of the cold water pipe should be 5.____

   A. the same
   B. twice as great
   C. one and one-half times as great
   D. one half as great

6. If the pitch of a horizontal steam line is 1/2 inch in 10 feet, one end of a 45-foot steam line is lower than the other end by, MOST NEARLY, _____ inches. 6.____

   A. 2   B. 2 1/4   C. 3   D. 3 1/2

7. A pump that removes 30 gallons of water per minute is pumping water from a cellar 30 feet x 50 feet covered with eight inches of water. One cubic foot of water equals 7.5 gallons of water.
   The number of minutes it will take to remove the eight inches of water from the cellar is, MOST NEARLY, 7.____

   A. 200   B. 225   C. 250   D. 275

8. Oil preheaters are used to 8.____

   A. economize on fuel oil
   B. reduce friction in the oil blower
   C. improve the flow of oil
   D. reduce oil volatility

27

9. The *FIRST* item which should be checked when a sump pit overflows because the automatic electric sump pump is not operating properly is the

   A. feedwater pressure
   B. ficat switch mechanism
   C. stat switch
   D. discharge line check valve

10. Chloride of lime should be used for the removal of

    A. alkali stains on wood
    B. grass stains on wood or marble
    C. indelible pencil and marking ink stains on concrete or terrazzo
    D. ink stains on wood

11. Of the following, the lack of a vapor barrier on the inside surface of a well-insulated wall may eventually cause, during the winter,

    A. plugging of weep holes
    B. peeling of exterior paint
    C. lower heat losses through the wall
    D. improvement in insulation performance by plugging air spaces with the insulation

12. When cold water pipes in a room *sweat*, it is USUALLY due to the

    A. surface of the pipes being below the dew point temperature of the room air
    B. specific humidity exceeding the relative humidity
    C. air in the room exceeding 100% relative humidity
    D. surface of the pipe being below the wet bulb temperature of the room air

13. The *MAIN* reason for applying floor finish to a floor surface is to

    A. protect against germs
    B. protect the floor surface
    C. increase traction
    D. waterproof the floor

14. The *MAIN* reason for preventing sewer gas from entering buildings through the plumbing system is because the gas

    A. is highly inflammable and explosive in nature and could result in a fire hazard
    B. has an eroding effect on plumbing fixtures and pipe lines
    C. is highly infectious and contagious in nature
    D. has a nuisance effect on occupants

15. The one of the following that is a concrete floor sealer is

    A. sodium silicate
    B. neatsfoot oil
    C. sodium hydroxide
    D. linseed oil

16. To help plants survive the shock of transplanting, in most cases, it is BEST to

    A. spray them with insecticide every day for a week
    B. cover the foliage with burlap for a day or two
    C. shade them from the sun for a week or two
    D. prune them every day for a week or two

17. When cutting a branch off a tree, it is desirable to undercut because it will

   A. prevent the weight of the branch from tearing off bark and wood below the cut
   B. make the tree grow stronger and straighter
   C. let the saw work smoother and easier
   D. make it easier to cut up the limb

18. The *MAIN* reason for applying lime to soil is to control its

   A. aridity   B. fertilization
   C. acidity   D. porosity

19. The *GREATEST* danger to a tree from a large unprotected wound is that

   A. birds may build a nest in it
   B. the tree may bleed to death
   C. the wound may become infected
   D. it is open to the elements

20. The fertilizer that is used for the care of trees should have a high content of

   A. DDT   B. nitrogen   C. sulphur   D. carbon

21. The area of the plot plan shown below is _____ square feet.

   A. 25,300
   B. 26,700
   C. 28,100
   D. 30,500

   (Dimensions: 270', 70', 150', 155', 115')

22. The *BEST* of the following combinations of instruments to use in checking the combustion efficiency of a heating boiler is

   A. anemometer, stack thermometer, and orsat apparatus
   B. draft gage, psychrometer, and barometer
   C. draft gage, stack thermometer, and orsat apparatus
   D. draft gage, stack thermometer, and barometer

23. The one of the following that does NOT indicate low water in a steam boiler is the

   A. fusible plug   B. safety valve
   C. tri cocks   D. gauge glass

24. The increase in the stack temperature toward the end of the heating system above what it was at the beginning of the season is an indication that the

   A. radiators and convectors are air bound
   B. tubes and heating surfaces of the boiler are becoming insulated with soot
   C. furnace fire brick is failing
   D. heat content of the fuel is improving

25. Of the following, the one which is NOT a general class of oil burners is the _____ atomizing.

    A. water   B. rotary cup   C. mechanical   D. air

26. Of the following, the one which should be between a boiler and its safety valve is

    A. a swing check valve of a size larger than that of the safety valve
    B. a butterfly valve located in the boiler-nozzle
    C. a gate valve of the same nominal size as that of the safety valve
    D. no valve of any type

27. The term *spinner cup* refers to

    A. screw-type stokers   B. gun-type oil burners
    C. rotary-type oil burners   D. chain grate stokers

28. A *gun-type* burner is often used on a

    A. pot-type oil burner
    B. low pressure gas boiler
    C. coal underfeed stoker boiler
    D. high pressure oil-fired boiler

29. Of the following, the action that should be taken as the FIRST step if a properly adjusted safety valve on a steam boiler *pops off* when in operation is

    A. open the-draft   B. add more water to the boiler
    C. wire the valve shut   D. reduce the draft

30. When the water gets below the safe level in an operating boiler, it is BEST to

    A. add new water up to the safe level and open up the fire so that the water will heat quickly
    B. check the fire and let the boiler cool down before new water is added
    C. add new water to the boiler immediately
    D. check the fire and empty the boiler

31. Vents on fuel oil storage tanks are used to

    A. fill the fuel tanks
    B. allow air to escape during filling
    C. check oil flash points
    D. make tank fuel soundings

32. Of the following, the MOST desirable way to remove carbon deposits from the atomizing cup of an oil burner is to

    A. apply a hot flame to the carbonized surfaces to burn off the carbon deposits
    B. use kerosene to loosen the deposits and wipe with a soft cloth
    C. wash the cup with a mild trisodium phosphate solution and dry with a cloth
    D. use a scraper, followed by light rubbing with emery cloth

33. Of the following, the MOST important precaution that should be taken when *cutting in* a boiler in a battery is to see that the

    A. water column is at least 1 inch below top row of tubes
    B. non-return valve is closed when the boiler pressure is rising
    C. safety valves function properly
    D. boiler pressure is about equal to header pressure

34. A condensate feedwater tank in a low pressure steam plant

    A. is hermetically sealed to prevent contamination of feed water
    B. contains a surface blow down line
    C. is vented to the atmosphere
    D. has a vacuum breaker exposed to the atmosphere

35. Of the following, the FIRST action to take in the event a low pressure steam boiler gauge glass breaks is to

    A. bank the fires
    B. close the water gauge glass cocks
    C. open the safety valve
    D. blow down the boiler

36. A *barometric damper* would be used in a boiler installation fired under draft conditions that are called

    A. induced   B. natural   C. regenerate   D. forced

37. The flue gas temperature, when firing oil, should be just high enough to evaporate any contained moisture in order to

    A. prevent an acid from forming and eroding the breeching
    B. decrease the amount of excess air needed
    C. prevent an air pollution condition
    D. lower the combustion efficiency of the boiler

38. A compound gauge in a boiler room

    A. measures pressures above and below atmospheric pressure
    B. indicates the degree of compounding in a steam engine
    C. shows the quantity of boiler treatment compound on hand
    D. measures steam and water pressure

39. In the combustion of the common fuels, the PRINCIPAL boiler heat loss is that due to the heat

    A. carried away by the moisture in the fuel
    B. lost by radiation
    C. carried away by the flue gases
    D. lost by incomplete combustion

40. Of the following, the CORRECT sequence of steps to use when removing a boiler from service in order to perform extensive repairs on it is   40._____

    A. discontinue firing, drain boiler, turn off valves, cool boiler
    B. discontinue firing, drain boiler, turn off valves
    C. turn off valves, drain boiler, discontinue firing, cool boiler
    D. discontinue firing, turn off valves, cool boiler, drain boiler

KEY (CORRECT ANSWERS)

1. C	11. B	21. C	31. B
2. B	12. A	22. C	32. B
3. D	13. B	23. B	33. D
4. C	14. D	24. B	34. C
5. A	15. A	25. A	35. B
6. B	16. C	26. D	36. B
7. C	17. A	27. C	37. A
8. C	18. C	28. D	38. A
9. B	19. C	29. D	39. C
10. C	20. B	30. B	40. D

TEST 2

DIRECTIONS: Each question or incomplete statement is followed by several suggested answers or completions. Select the one that BEST answers the question or completes the statement. *PRINT THE LETTER OF THE CORRECT ANSWER IN THE SPACE AT THE RIGHT.*

1. With the same outdoor winter temperatures, the load on a heating boiler starting up is greater than the normal morning load MAINLY because of

   A. loss of heat escaping through the stack
   B. steam required to heat boiler water and piping to radiators
   C. viscosity of the fuel oil
   D. low outdoor temperatures

   1.____

2. The FIRST operation when starting a boiler after it has been on bank overnight should be to

   A. blow down the boiler
   B. clean the furnace
   C. check the gate valves
   D. look at the water gauge and try the gauge cocks

   2.____

3. *Cascading* of raw city water when filling a cleaned boiler should be avoided because it

   A. is harmful to the mud drum
   B. adds additional free oxygen in the boiler
   C. adds considerable time to the filling procedure
   D. will stress tube and sheet joints

   3.____

4. The average temperature on a day in January was 24° F. The number of degree-days for that day was

   A. 12   B. 24   C. 41   D. 48

   4.____

5. Under normal conditions during the growing season, lawns should receive a good saturation of water with a spray

   A. once a day   B. once a week
   C. once a month   D. twice a month

   5.____

6. One of the important benefits to floors that wax does NOT provide is

   A. easier soil removal   B. improved stain resistance
   C. reduction in wear   D. resistance to fire

   6.____

7. In the Ringelmann chart of smoke density, number 4 indicates

   A. the darkest smoke condition
   B. the lightest smoke condition
   C. smoke density of 80 per cent
   D. no smoke condition

   7.____

8. Of the following, the estinguishing agent that should be used on fires in flammable liquids is

   A. steam   B. water   C. foam   D. soda and acid

9. A soda-acid fire extinguisher is recommended for use on fires consisting of

   A. wood or paper
   B. fuel oil or gasoline
   C. electrical causes or fuel oil
   D. paint or turpentine

10. The *CHIEF* reason wooden ladders should *NOT* be painted is that the paint may

    A. hide defects
    B. mark up the walls
    C. make the ladder slippery
    D. damage the rungs

11. In accordance with the uniform method of identifying piping in public buildings, pipes carrying materials classified as being dangerous are colored

    A. blue
    B. red
    C. orange and yellow
    D. green and white

12. The *MOST* effective way to eliminate fire hazards in public buildings is to

    A. hold frequent fire drills
    B. have the fire department inspect the building annually
    C. promote constant self-inspection
    D. supply each building with ample fire fighting equipment

13. When a room is air conditioned in the summer, the windows should be

    A. opened at the top and bottom to improve circulation
    B. screened to keep out the dirt
    C. kept closed
    D. opened at the top only to let hot air escape

14. In order to clean an office with 20,000 sq. ft. of space in four hours, using a standard of 900 sq. ft. per hour, the number of cleaners you should assign to do the job is *MOST NEARLY*

    A. 4   B. 6   C. 8   D. 10

15. The area of a floor 35' wide and 45' long is, in square yards, *MOST NEARLY*

    A. 175   B. 262   C. 525   D. 1575

16. A pyrometer is an instrument used for measuring

    A. condensation and humidity
    B. high temperatures
    C. noise pollution
    D. water flow

17. It is usually desirable to assign the cleaning of an office to one employee only because

    A. the amount of time wasted through talking is decreased
    B. an employee working alone, by himself, is more efficient
    C. there is no question who is responsible for the work done
    D. working alone reduces the rate and severity of accidents

18. Of each dollar spent on the cleaning of public buildings, the amount spent on cleaning supplies is usually not more than _____ cents.

    A. 5   B. 35   C. 55   D. 75

19. Of the following solutions, the one MOST often used in washing exterior glass is _____ water and a small quantity of _____.

    A. cold; turpentine
    B. cold; ammonia
    C. cold; glass wax
    D. warm; soft soap

20. Rust stains in wash basins can BEST be prevented by

    A. applying wax film to the rusty surface
    B. replacing leaking faucet washers
    C. adding rust inhibitor to the domestic cold water storage tank
    D. sand papering the rusty surfaces

21. Of the following, the one which is likely to be MOST harmful to asphalt tile is

    A. coffee   B. ketchup   C. salad oil   D. vinegar

22. Of the following, when sweeping a corridor with a floor brush, the cleaner should

    A. lean on the brush and walk the length of the corridor
    B. give the brush a slight jerk after each stroke to free it of loose dirt
    C. make certain there is no overlap on sweeping strokes
    D. use moderately long pull strokes

23. Time standards for cleaning are of value ONLY if

    A. a bonus is promised if the time standards are beaten
    B. the cleaners determine the methods and procedures to be used
    C. accompanied by a completely detailed description of the methods to be used
    D. a schematic diagram of the area is made available to the cleaners

24. Of the following, the one which is the LEAST important factor in deciding that additional training is necessary for the men you supervise is that

    A. the quality of work is below standard
    B. supplies are being wasted
    C. too much time is required to do specific jobs
    D. the absentee rate has declined

25. To promote proper safety practices in the operation of power tools and equipment, you should emphasize in meetings with the staff that

    A. every accident can be prevented through proper safety regulations
    B. proper safety practices will probably make future safety meetings unnecessary

C. when safety rules are followed, tools and equipment will work better
D. safety rules are based on past experience with the best methods of preventing accidents

26. A good practical method to use in determining whether an employee is doing his job properly is to

   A. assume that if he asks no questions, he knows the work
   B. question him directly on details of the job
   C. inspect and follow up the work which is assigned to him
   D. ask other employees how this employee is making out

27. If an employee continually asks how he should do his work, you should

   A. dismiss him immediately
   B. pretend you do not hear him unless he persists
   C. explain the work carefully but encourage him to use his own judgment
   D. tell him not to ask so many questions

28. You have instructed an employee to wet-mop a certain area. To be sure that the employee understands the instructions you have given him, you should

   A. ask him to repeat the instructions to you
   B. check with him after he has done the job
   C. watch him while he is doing the job
   D. repeat the instructions to the employee

29. One of your men disagrees with your evaluation of his work.
    Of the following, the BEST way to handle this situation would be to

   A. explain that you are in a better position to evaluate his work than he is
   B. tell him that since other men are satisfied with your evaluation, he should accept their opinions
   C. explain the basis of your evaluation and discuss it with him
   D. refuse to discuss his complaint in order to maintain discipline

30. Of the following, the one which is NOT a quality of leadership desirable in a supervisor is

   A. intelligence   B. integrity
   C. forcefulness   D. partiality

31. Of the following, the one which LEAST characterizes the *grapevine* is that it

   A. consists of a tremendous amount of rumor, conjecture, information, advice, prediction, and even orders
   B. seems to rise spontaneously, is largely anonymous, spreads rapidly, and changes in unpredictable directions
   C. can be eliminated without any great effort
   D. commonly fills the gaps left by the regular organizational channels of communication

32. Of the following, the one which is NOT a purpose of a cleaning job breakdown is to

   A. eliminate unnecessary steps
   B. determine the type of floor wax to use

C. rearrange the sequence of operations to save time
D. combine steps or actions where practicable

33. Of the following, the *PRINCIPAL* function of a supervisor is to

    A. train and instruct his subordinates in the proper methods of doing their work
    B. eliminate all accidents
    C. prepare reports on his activities to his supervisor
    D. prepare a thorough job methods analysis

34. The *BEST* method of making cleaning assignments in a large building is by means of

    A. daily rotation
    B. specific assignment
    C. individual choice
    D. chronological order

35. When one of your new cleaning employees is making little progress after the usual training period with one of your experienced men, you should

    A. recommend to your superior that he should be discharged
    B. tell your superior he is not interested in the job
    C. determine the reason for the poor results
    D. discontinue all training

36. For a supervisor to have his cleaning employees willing to follow standardized cleaning procedures, he must be prepared to

    A. associate with his employees
    B. show that the procedures are reasonable
    C. give extra time off
    D. set up a penalty system

37. One of the employees you supervise has broken the rule against keeping liquor in his locker.
    You should

    A. make believe it never happened and forget the incident
    B. explain the rule to him and that a repetition may result in disciplinary action
    C. suspend him immediately
    D. fire him immediately

38. The *BEST* action for you to take on receiving complaints of poor illumination in one of the offices is to

    A. wait until you have several complaints of this kind
    B. tell the complainant nothing can be done
    C. request that additional ceiling lights be installed
    D. check the office for the cause of poor illumination

39. The *MAIN* purpose of periodic inspections and tests of mechanical equipment is to

    A. keep the men busy during otherwise slack periods
    B. discover minor faults before they develop into major faults
    C. make the men familiar with the equipment
    D. encourage the men to take better care of the equipment

40. Assume that one of your employees has been slightly injured while doing a cleaning job. After the employee has been cared for, you should NEXT
   A. investigate the cause of the accident
   B. notify the union
   C. charge the employee with recklessness
   D. transfer the employee

KEY (CORRECT ANSWERS)

1. B	11. C	21. C	31. C
2. D	12. C	22. B	32. B
3. B	13. C	23. C	33. A
4. C	14. B	24. D	34. B
5. B	15. A	25. D	35. C
6. D	16. B	26. C	36. B
7. C	17. C	27. C	37. B
8. C	18. A	28. A	38. D
9. A	19. B	29. C	39. B
10. A	20. B	30. D	40. A

EXAMINATION SECTION
TEST 1

DIRECTIONS: Each question or incomplete statement is followed by several suggested answers or completions. Select the one that BEST answers the question or completes the statement. *PRINT THE LETTER OF THE CORRECT ANSWER IN THE SPACE AT THE RIGHT.*

1. Linseed oil is MOST commonly used to

   A. seal wooden floors
   B. polish brass fixtures
   C. thin exterior oil base paints
   D. lubricate fan bearings

2. The APPROXIMATE number of square feet of unobstructed corridor floorspace that one cleaner can sweep in an hour is

   A. 1200   B. 2400   C. 4000   D. 6000

3. Of the following materials, the one MOST effective in dusting office furniture is a

   A. silk cloth   B. chamois
   C. soft cotton cloth   D. counter brush

4. Of the following materials, the one that should be used to produce the MOST resilient flooring is

   A. concrete   B. terrazzo
   C. ceramic tile   D. asphalt tile

5. Sweeping compound is used on concrete floors MAINLY to

   A. keep the dust down
   B. polish the floor
   C. harden the floor surface
   D. indicate which part of the floor has not been swept

6. The type of floor finish or wax that will produce an anti-slip surface on resilient floor coverings is

   A. resin-based floor finish
   B. water emulsion wax
   C. paste wax
   D. paraffin

7. High sheen and good wearing qualities can be obtained when polishing a waxed floor by using an electric scrubbing machine equipped with

   A. nylon disks   B. soft brushes
   C. steel wool pads   D. pumice wheels

8. Spalling of the surface of a marble floor may result if the floor is washed with

   A. a solution of trisodium phosphate   B. a soft soap solution
   C. a neutral liquid detergent solution D. cold water

9. When not in use, a broom should be stored

   A. resting on the floor with the handle end down
   B. resting on the floor with the bristle end down
   C. hanging by the handle from a hook
   D. lying flat on the floor

10. The one of the following items which ordinarily requires the MOST time to wash is a(n)

    A. 5 ft x 10 ft Venetian blind
    B. 4 ft fluorescent fixture
    C. incandescent fixture
    D. 5 ft x 10 ft ceramic tile floor

11. A broom that has been properly used should GENERALLY be replaced after

    A. it has been used for one month
    B. its bristles have been worn down by more than one-third of their original length
    C. it has been used for two months
    D. its bristles have been worn down by more than two-thirds of their original length

12. The floor area of a room which measures 10 ft long x 10 ft wide is _____ sq. ft.

    A. 20   B. 40   C. 100   D. 1000

13. The FIRST thing that should be checked before an oil-fired, low-pressure steam boiler is started up in the morning is the

    A. boiler water level   B. stack temperature
    C. aquastat   D. vaporstat

14. The MAIN reason for preheating number 6 fuel oil before allowing it to enter an oil burner is to

    A. increase its viscosity
    B. decrease its viscosity
    C. increase its heating value
    D. decrease its flash point

15. A house pump is used to

    A. drain basements that become flooded
    B. pump sewage from the basement to the sewer
    C. pump city water to a roof storage tank
    D. circulate domestic hot water

16. The device which shuts down an automatic rotary cup oil burner when the steam pressure reaches a preset high limit is a

    A. pressure gage   B. pressurtrol
    C. safety valve   D. low water cutoff

17. A pressure gage connected to a compressed air tank USUALLY reads in

    A. pounds
    B. pounds per square inch
    C. inches of mercury
    D. feet of water

18. The device which shuts off the oil burner when the water level in the boiler is too low is the

    A. feedwater regulator
    B. low water cutoff
    C. high water alarm
    D. programmer

19. The device which shuts down an oil burner when there is a flame failure is the

    A. stack switch
    B. thermostat
    C. manometer
    D. modutrol motor

20. The switch which is used to shut off the oil burner in case of a fire in the boiler room is located

    A. on the programmer cover
    B. near the boiler room entrance
    C. on the burner motor
    D. in the custodian's office

21. The MOST likely reason for a cold water faucet to continue to drip after its washer has been replaced is a defective

    A. handle   B. stem   C. seat   D. bib

22. In water lines, the type of valve which should always be either fully open or fully closed is the

    A. needle valve
    B. gate valve
    C. globe valve
    D. mixing valve

23. The BEST tool to use on a 1" galvanized iron pipe nipple when unscrewing the nipple from a coupling is a _____ wrench.

    A. crescent   B. stillson   C. monkey   D. spud

24. The BEST way to locate a leak in a natural gas pipe line is to

    A. hold a lighted match under the pipe and move it along the length of the pipe slowly
    B. hold a lighted match about two inches above the pipe and move it along the length of the pipe slowly
    C. coat the pipe with a soapy solution and watch for bubbles
    D. shut off the gas at the meter and then coat the pipe with a soapy solution and watch for bubbles

25. When comparing a 60 watt yellow bulb with a 60 watt clear bulb, it can be said that they BOTH

    A. give the same amount of light
    B. use the same amount of power
    C. will burn for at least 60 hours
    D. will burn for at least 60 days

26. The output capacity of an electric motor is USUALLY rated in 26.____

    A. kilowatts   B. horsepower
    C. percent   D. cubic feet

27. A fuse will burn out whenever it is subjected to excessive 27.____

    A. resistance   B. voltage
    C. current   D. capacitance

28. Of the following, the device which uses the GREATEST amount of electric power is the 28.____

    A. electric typewriter
    B. $\frac{1}{4}$ inch electric drill
    C. floor scrubbing machine
    D. oil burner ignition transformer

29. Meters which indicate the electric power consumed in a public building are read in 29.____

    A. kilowatt-hours   B. volts
    C. cubic feet   D. degree days

30. Tongue and groove lumber is used for 30.____

    A. desk drawers   B. hardwood floors
    C. picture frames   D. cabinet doors

31. When hand sawing a 1" x 4" board parallel to the grain of the wood, the BEST saw to use is the _____ saw. 31.____

    A. cross-cut   B. back
    C. hack   D. rip

32. The BEST tool to use to make a recess for the head of a flat-head wood screw is a(n) 32.____

    A. counterbore   B. countersink
    C. auger   D. nail set

33. In attaching two pieces of wood with a nut and bolt, the holes drilled should be 33.____

    A. slightly undersize in one piece, slightly oversize in the other
    B. slightly oversize in both pieces
    C. slightly undersize in both pieces
    D. drilled from opposite sides of the joint

34. The one of the following transmission devices which should be oiled MOST often is the 34.____

    A. V-belt   B. roller chain
    C. rigid coupling   D. clutch plate

35. A motor-generator set is USUALLY part of a(n) 35.____

    A. steam boiler   B. hydraulic elevator
    C. electric elevator   D. incinerator

36. The one of the following devices which MOST frequently contains hydraulic fluid is a   36.____

    A. door closer
    B. worm gear reducer
    C. foam fire extinguisher
    D. hand winch

37. A breakdown of the causes of accidental injuries by percent would show that such injuries are *most nearly* caused   37.____

    A. 100 percent by unsafe physical working conditions
    B. 100 percent by unsafe acts of people
    C. 50 percent by unsafe physical working conditions and 50 percent by unsafe acts of people
    D. 20 percent by unsafe physical working conditions and 80 percent by unsafe acts of people

38. When using an eight-foot stepladder, a worker should climb up not more than _____ rungs.   38.____

    A. 4   B. 5   C. 6   D. 7

39. A supervisor interested in the safety of his subordinates would NOT permit   39.____

    A. using a wooden rule to take measurements near electrical apparatus
    B. using a machinist's hammer to strike a chisel
    C. removing metal chips from a machine with a rag
    D. testing the heat of a soldering iron with a piece of solder

40. If a worker feels an electric shock while using a portable electric drill, he should immediately   40.____

    A. stand on a piece of scrap lumber
    B. reverse the plug in the receptacle
    C. hold onto a grounded pipe or piece of metal
    D. take the drill out of service

KEY (CORRECT ANSWERS)

1. C	11. B	21. C	31. D
2. D	12. C	22. B	32. B
3. C	13. A	23. B	33. B
4. D	14. A	24. C	34. B
5. A	15. C	25. B	35. C
6. A	16. B	26. B	36. A
7. B	17. B	27. C	37. D
8. A	18. B	28. C	38. C
9. C	19. A	29. A	39. C
10. A	20. B	30. B	40. D

TEST 2

DIRECTIONS: Each question or incomplete statement is followed by several suggested answers or completions. Select the one that BEST answers the question or completes the statement. *PRINT THE LETTER OF THE CORRECT ANSWER IN THE SPACE AT THE RIGHT.*

1. During a shortage of custodial help in a public building, the cleaning task which will probably receive LEAST attention is   1.____

    A. picking up sweepings
    B. emptying ashtrays
    C. washing walls
    D. dust-mopping offices

2. Of the following substances commonly used on floors, the MOST flammable is   2.____

    A. resin-based floor finish
    B. floor sealer
    C. water emulsion wax
    D. trisodium phosphate

3. The MOST effective method for cleaning badly soiled carpeting is   3.____

    A. wet shampooing
    B. vacuum cleaning
    C. dry shampooing
    D. wire brushing

4. Before repainting becomes necessary, a painted wall can USUALLY be washed completely   4.____

    A. only once
    B. two or three times
    C. eight to ten times
    D. sixteen to twenty times

5. The FIRST step in routine cleaning of offices at night should be   5.____

    A. sweeping floors
    B. emptying ashtrays
    C. dusting furniture
    D. damp mopping the floors

6. Among the factors pertaining to the maintenance and cleaning of a building, the one MOST likely to be under the control of the building custodian is the   6.____

    A. size of the area
    B. density of occupancy
    C. type of occupancy
    D. standards to be maintained

7. "Treated" or "dustless" sweeping of resilient-type floors requires   7.____

    A. spraying the floors with water to keep the dust down
    B. spreading sweeping compound on the floor
    C. sweeping cloths that are chemically treated with mineral oil
    D. spraying the sweeping tool with neatsfoot oil

8. A modern central vacuum cleaner system   8.____

    A. is cheaper to operate than one portable machine
    B. generally produces less suction than a portable machine
    C. conveys the dirt directly to a basement tank
    D. must be operated only in the daytime

9. Oxalic acid can be used to

   A. remove ink spots from wood
   B. clear floor drains
   C. solder copper flashing
   D. polish brass

10. The BEST material for sealing a terrazzo floor is

    A. varnish
    B. a penetrating seal
    C. shellac
    D. a surface seal

11. The MOST troublesome feature in cleaning public washrooms is

    A. cleaning and deodorizing the urinals
    B. washing the toilet bowls
    C. mopping the tile floors
    D. removing chewing gum from the floors

12. In order to improve its appearance, extend its life, and reduce the labor involved in dusting, wood furniture should be polished with

    A. an oil polish
    B. a water emulsion wax
    C. a silicone and spirit chemical spray
    D. clear water

13. Ringelmann charts are useful in determining

    A. interest rates
    B. smoke density
    C. standard times for cleaning operations
    D. fuel consumption

14. A fusible plug is USUALLY found in a

    A. lighting panel
    B. fire door
    C. boiler wall
    D. house tank

15. In an air conditioned office, MOST people would feel comfortable when the room temperature and humidity are maintained, respectively, at

    A. 75° F and 50%
    B. 70° F and 30%
    C. 75° F and 20%
    D. 65° F and 75%

16. The one of the following sets of conditions which will provide the MOST efficient combustion in an oil-fired low-temperature steam boiler is _____ stack temperature, _____ CO_2.

    A. 400° F, 12%
    B. 500° F, 10%
    C. 600° F, 8%
    D. 700° F, 6%

17. The BEST way for a building custodian to tell if the night cleaners have done their work well is to check   17.___

    A. on how much cleaning material has been used
    B. on how much waste paper was collected
    C. the building for cleanliness
    D. the floor mops to see if they are still wet

18. The one of the following which is the BEST reason for introducing a training program is that the   18.___

    A. quality of work is above standard
    B. employees are all experienced
    C. accident rate is too high
    D. tenant complaints are negligible

19. The FIRST step in training an inexperienced individual in a particular job is to   19.___

    A. put him to work and watch for mistakes
    B. put him to work and tell him to call for help if he needs it
    C. put him at ease and then find out what he knows about the work
    D. tell him to watch the least experienced worker on the job because the training is still fresh in his mind

20. As used in job analysis, the term "job breakdown" means   20.___

    A. any equipment failure
    B. any failure on the part of the worker to complete the job
    C. dividing the job into a series of steps
    D. reducing the number of workers by 50 percent

21. At times when a public building is closed to the public, the building custodian should   21.___

    A. keep all doors locked and admit no one
    B. admit only custodial employees
    C. admit anyone as long as he signs the log
    D. admit only those who have business in the building

22. When a public building is equipped for security purposes with exterior lights on or around the building, the lights should be kept lit   22.___

    A. all night except for Saturdays, Sundays, and holidays
    B. twenty-four hours a day on weekends
    C. throughout the night, every night of the week
    D. until midnight, every night of the week

23. Custodial workers are MOST liable to injury when they are engaged in   23.___

    A. sweeping floors   B. mopping floors
    C. dusting furniture   D. moving furniture

24. The BEST place to store a wooden stepladder is 24._____

    A. in a boiler room
    B. in a stairwell
    C. in a dry room
    D. outside a basement window provided that there is a locked grating overhead

25. Of the following, the BEST action for a building custodian to take when he notices that an office worker in his building has a hot plate connected to a heavily loaded electric circuit is to 25._____

    A. remove the hot plate from the office when its owner is not present
    B. demand that the office worker remove the hot plate immediately
    C. write a report to the supervisor of the office requesting corrective action
    D. ignore the situation

26. In dealing with the public, a building custodian should be 26._____

    A. indulgent   B. courteous
    C. disagreeable   D. unavailable

27. If a building custodian sees a group of people in front of his building preparing to form a picket line, he should 27._____

    A. turn on a lawn sprinkler to spray the pickets
    B. order the pickets off the sidewalk in front of the building
    C. show the pickets he is sympathetic with their complaint
    D. contact his supervisor immediately for instructions

28. When electric service in a public building is to be shut off from 10 A.M. Tuesday to 11:30 the next morning because a new electric feeder cable is being installed, the building custodian should 28._____

    A. prepare a memo to all office supervisors in the building, notifying them of the situation, and deliver a copy to each office as soon as possible
    B. prepare a notice of the impending power stoppage and post it in the lobby early Tuesday morning
    C. tell the electrical contractor to notify the tenants when he is about to shut off the power
    D. discontinue elevator service at 10 A.M. on Tuesday as an indication to the tenants that the power supply is off

29. The BEST way to remove some small pieces of broken glass from a floor is to 29._____

    A. use a brush and dustpan
    B. pick up the pieces carefully with your hands
    C. use a wet mop and a wringer
    D. sweep the pieces into the corner of the room

30. There is a two-light fixture in the room where you are working. One of the light bulbs goes out, and you need more light to work by. You should 30._____

    A. change the fuse in the fuse box
    B. have a new bulb put in
    C. call for an electrician and stop work till he comes
    D. find out what is causing the short circuit

31. While working on the job, you accidently break a window pane. No one is around, and you are able to clean up the broken pieces of glass. It would then be BEST for you to

   A. leave a note near the window that a new glass has to be put in because it was accidently broken
   B. forget about the whole thing because the window was not broken on purpose
   C. write a report to your supervisor telling him that you saw a broken window pane that has to be fixed
   D. tell your supervisor that you accidently broke the window pane while working

32. Many machines have certain safety devices for the operators. The MOST important reason for having these safety devices is to

   A. increase the amount of work that the machines can do
   B. permit repairs to be made on the machines without shutting them down
   C. help prevent accidents to people who use the machines
   D. reduce the cost of electric power needed to run the machines

Questions 33-36.

DIRECTIONS: Answer Questions 33 through 36 only according to the information given in the following passage.

MOPPING FLOORS

When mopping hardened cement floors, either painted or unpainted, a soap and water mixture should be used. This should be made by dissolving 1/2 a cup of soft soap in a pail of hot water. It is not desirable, however, under any circumstances, to use a soap and water mixture on cement floors that are not hardened. For mopping this type of floor, it is recommended that the cleaning agent be made up of 2 ounces of laundry soda mixed in a pail of water.

Soaps are not generally used on hard tile floors because slippery films may build up on the floor. It is generally recommended that these floors be mopped using a pail of hot water in which has been mixed 2 ounces of washing powder for each gallon of water. The floors should then be rinsed thoroughly.

After the mopping is finished, proper care should be taken of the mop. This is done by first cleaning the mop in clear warm water. Then it should be wrung out, after which the strands of the mop should be untangled. Finally, the mop should be hung by its handle to dry.

33. According to the above passage, you should NEVER use a soap and water mixture when mopping _____ floors.

   A. hardened cement   B. painted
   C. unhardened cement   D. unpainted

34. According to the above passage, using laundry soda mixed in a pail of water as a cleaning agent is recommended for

   A. all floors
   B. all floors except hard tile floors
   C. some cement floors
   D. linoleum floor coverings only

35. According to the above passage, the GENERALLY recommended mixture for mopping hard tile floors is

   A. 1/2 cup of soft soap for each gallon of hot water
   B. 1/2 cup of soft soap in a pail of hot water
   C. 2 ounces of washing powder in a pail of hot water
   D. 2 ounches of washing powder for each gallon of hot water

36. According to the above passage, the PROPER care of a mop after it is used includes

   A. cleaning it in clear cold water and hanging it by its handle to dry
   B. wringing it out, untangling, and drying it
   C. untangling its strands before wringing it out
   D. untangling its strands while cleaning it in clear water

Questions 37-40.

DIRECTIONS: Answer Questions 37 through 40 only according to the information given in the following passage.

ACCIDENT PREVENTION

Many accidents and injuries can be prevented if employees learn to be move careful. The wearing of shoes with thin or badly worn soles or open toes can easily lead to foot injuries from tacks, nails, and chair and desk legs. Loose or torn clothing should not be worn near moving machinery. This is especially true of neckties which can very easily become caught in the machine. You should not place objects so that they block or partly block hallways, corridors, or other passageways. Even when they are stored in the proper place, tools, supplies, and equipment should be carefully placed or piled so as not to fall, nor have anything stick out from a pile. Before cabinets, lockers or ladders are moved, the tops should be cleared of anything which might injure someone or fall off. If necessary, use a dolly to move these or other bulky objects.

Despite all efforts to avoid accidents and injuries, however, some will happen. If an employee is injured, no matter how small the injury, he should report it to his supervisor and have the injury treated. A small cut that is not attended to can easily become infected and can cause more trouble than some injuries which at first seem more serious. It never pays to take chances.

37. According to the above passage, the one statement that is NOT true is that

   A. by being more careful, employees can reduce the number of accidents that happen
   B. women should wear shoes with open toes for comfort when working
   C. supplies should be piled so that nothing is sticking out from the pile
   D. if an employee sprains his wrist at work, he should tell his supervisor about it

38. According to the above passage, you should NOT wear loose clothing when you are

   A. in a corridor
   B. storing tools
   C. opening cabinets
   D. near moving machinery

39. According to the above passage, before moving a ladder, you should 39.____
    A. test all the rungs
    B. get a dolly to carry the ladder at all times
    C. remove everything from the top of the ladder which might fall off
    D. remove your necktie

40. According to the above passage, an employee who gets a slight cut should 40.____
    A. have it treated to help prevent infection
    B. know that a slight cut becomes more easily infected than a big cut
    C. pay no attention to it as it can't become serious
    D. realize that it is more serious than any other type of injury

KEY (CORRECT ANSWERS)

1. C	11. A	21. D	31. D
2. B	12. C	22. C	32. C
3. A	13. B	23. D	33. C
4. B	14. C	24. C	34. C
5. B	15. A	25. C	35. D
6. D	16. A	26. B	36. B
7. C	17. C	27. D	37. B
8. C	18. C	28. A	38. D
9. A	19. C	29. A	39. C
10. B	20. C	30. B	40. A

TEST 3

DIRECTIONS: Each question or incomplete statement is followed by several suggested answers or completions. Select the one that BEST answers the question or completes the statement. *PRINT THE LETTER OF THE CORRECT ANSWER IN THE SPACE AT THE RIGHT.*

1. An electric motor fire should be put out with an extinguisher that uses   1.____
   - A. carbon dioxide
   - B. soda-acid
   - C. foam
   - D. a pump tank

2. The charge in a soda-acid fire extinguisher should be replaced once   2.____
   - A. a month
   - B. every three months
   - C. every six months
   - D. a year

3. An elevator machinery room should have a fire extinguisher of the _____ type.   3.____
   - A. soda-acid
   - B. foam
   - C. carbon dioxide
   - D. sand pail

4. The national flag should be raised   4.____
   - A. slowly and lowered briskly
   - B. briskly and lowered slowly
   - C. briskly and lowered briskly
   - D. slowly and lowered slowly

5. The material which is used to seal the outside edges of a pane of window glass is   5.____
   - A. stellite
   - B. putty
   - C. plastic wood
   - D. caulking compound

6. The ceiling of a room which measures 20 ft x 30 ft is to be given two coats of paint. If one gallon of paint will cover 500 square feet, the two coats of paint will require a MINIMUM of _____ gallons.   6.____
   - A. 1.5
   - B. 2
   - C. 2.4
   - D. 3.2

7. Rubbish, sticks, and papers on the lawn in front of a building should be collected by using a   7.____
   - A. rake
   - B. broom
   - C. paper sticker
   - D. hoe

8. Mortar stains on brickwork can be scrubbed off by using a solution of   8.____
   - A. benzine
   - B. tri-sodium phosphate
   - C. muriatic acid
   - D. acetic acid

9. The BEST chemical for melting ice on sidewalks is   9.____
   - A. sodium chloride
   - B. calcium carbonate
   - C. hydrogen sulphide
   - D. calcium chloride

10. Before painting a kitchen wall,

    A. a degreaser must be mixed with the paint
    B. all traces of grease must be washed off
    C. a water-base paint must be used to dissolve the grease
    D. the walls must be sanded to remove all traces of grease and old paint

11. For interior walls which must be washed very often, the PREFERRED paint is

    A. enamel   B. flat
    C. exterior varnish   D. calsomine

12. A type of window which is USUALLY equipped with sash cords or chains is the _____ type.

    A. hopper   B. awning
    C. casement   D. double-hung

13. The slats of a Venetian blind are usually tilted by a device containing a _____ gear.

    A. worm   B. spur   C. hypoid   D. bevil

14. When washing the outside of a window with a narrow inside sill, a window cleaner should place his water pail on

    A. the outside window sill
    B. the nearest desk or chair
    C. a radiator at the center of the window
    D. the floor at a convenient point toward one side of the window

15. In order to determine the carrying capacity of a passenger elevator, a custodian would have to

    A. measure the floor area
    B. check the diameter of the cable
    C. read the inspection certificate
    D. read the motor nameplate

16. Before pruning a tree, the FIRST step should be to determine

    A. if there is insect infestation
    B. the general health of the tree
    C. the desired results
    D. amount of excess foliage

17. Tree fertilizer should have a high content of

    A. slaked lime   B. chlordane
    C. rose dust   D. nitrogen

18. A gasoline-driven snow blower should be stored for the summer with its fuel tank

    A. filled with gasoline
    B. and fuel lines drained
    C. filled with water
    D. half filled with number 4 fuel oil

19. A pipe that "sweats" in the summer time PROBABLY contains 19.____

    A. hot water B. low pressure steam
    C. domestic gas D. cold water

20. A good preventive maintenance program requires that each item of equipment be 20.____

    A. represented by an up-to-date record card on file
    B. lubricated daily
    C. brand new at the start of the program
    D. painted inside and out

Questions 21-24.

DIRECTIONS: Questions 21 through 24, inclusive, are to be answered SOLELY on the basis of the following paragraph.

All cleaning agents and supplies should be kept in a central storeroom which should be kept looked and only the custodian, storekeeper and foreman should have keys. Shelving should be provided for the smaller items, while barrels containing scouring powder or other bulk material should be set on the floor or on special cradles. Each compartment in the shelves should be marked plainly and only the item indicated stored therein. Each barrel should also be marked plainly. It may also be desirable to keep special items such as electric lamps, flashlight batteries, etc., in a locked cabinet or separate room to which only the custodian and the night building foreman have keys.

21. According to the above paragraph, scouring powder 21.____

    A. should be kept on shelves
    B. comes in one-pound cans
    C. should be kept in a locked cabinet
    D. is a bulk material

22. According to the above paragraph, 22.____

    A. the storekeeper should not be entrusted with the safekeeping of light bulbs
    B. flashlight batteries should be stored in barrels
    C. the central storeroom should be kept locked
    D. only special items should be stored under lock and key

23. According to the above paragraph, 23.____

    A. each shelf compartment should contain at least four different items
    B. barrels must be stored in cradles
    C. all items stored should be in marked compartments
    D. crates of light bulbs should be stored in cradles

24. As used in the above paragraph, the word *cradle* means a 24.____

    A. dolly B. support
    C. doll's bed D. hand truck

Questions 25-28.

DIRECTIONS: Questions 25 through 28, inclusive, are to be answered SOLELY on the basis of the following paragraph.

There are on the market many cleaning agents for which amazing claims are made. Chemical analysis shows that the majority of them are well-known chemicals slightly modified and packaged and sold under various trade names. For that reason, the agents which have been selected for your use are those whose cleaning properties are well-known and whose use can be standardized. It is obviously undesirable to offer too wide a selection as that would be confusing to the cleaner, but a sufficient number must be provided so that a satisfactory agent is available for each task.

25. According to the above paragraph,

    A. there are few cleaning agents on the market
    B. there are no really good cleaning agents on the market
    C. cleaning agents are sold under several different brand names
    D. all cleaning agents are the same

26. According to the above paragraph,

    A. all cleaning agents should be chemically analyzed before use
    B. the best cleaning agents are those for which no claims are made by the manufacturer
    C. different cleaning agents may be needed for different tasks
    D. all cleaning agents have been standardized by the federal government

27. As used in the above paragraph, the word *amazing* means

    A. illegal
    B. untrue
    C. astonishing
    D. specific

28. As used in the above paragraph, the word *modified* means

    A. changed
    B. refined
    C. labelled
    D. diluted

29. The MAIN reason for keeping an inventory of housekeeping supplies is to

    A. be sure that supplies are available when needed
    B. determine the cost of the supplies
    C. automatically prevent waste of the supplies
    D. be sure that at least two years' supplies are on hand at all times

30. Current daily records are MOST desirable in dealing with problems concerning

    A. accidents
    B. vandalism
    C. employee time and attendance
    D. the consumption of electricity

31. The continuous record of activities taking place in a boiler room is called a

    A. computer
    B. data bank
    C. log book
    D. time sheet

32. The one of the following subjects of a fire prevention training program which is MOST readily applied on the job is the

    A. elimination of fire hazards
    B. use of portable fire extinguishers
    C. knowledge of types of fires
    D. method of reporting fires

33. A good supervisor will NOT

    A. tell his men what their jobs are and why they are important
    B. show his men how their jobs are to be done in the right way
    C. require some of the men to do their jobs in the presence of the supervisor demonstrating that they understand the job
    D. leave his men alone because they will always do their jobs correctly once they have received their instructions

34. When a supervisor sees a worker doing his job incorrectly, he should

    A. tell the worker to be more careful
    B. suspend the worker until he learns to do the job correctly
    C. tell the worker specifically how the job should be done
    D. scold the man

35. An office worker complains to a custodian that one of the cleaners broke off a branch of a plant which she kept on her desk and that she can identify the cleaner.
    The BEST thing for the custodian to do is to

    A. convince her that the plant will grow another branch eventually
    B. make the cleaner apologize and pay for a new plant out of his own pocket
    C. sympathize with the office worker and assure her that he will speak to the cleaner about it
    D. tell her not to bother him about her personal property

36. An employee who is a good worker but is often late for work

    A. is lazy and should be dismissed
    B. cannot tell time
    C. can have no excuse for being late more than once a month
    D. should be questioned by his supervisor to try to find out why he is late

37. When starting any disciplinary action, a good supervisor should

    A. show his annoyance by losing his temper
    B. be apologetic
    C. be sarcastic
    D. be firm and positive

38. Good public relations can be damaged by a custodian who treats tenants, fellow workers, friends, relatives, and the public with

    A. courtesy
    B. consideration
    C. contempt
    D. respect

39. The BEST way for a supervisor to maintain good employee morale is to 39.____
    A. avoid praising any one employee
    B. always have an alibi for his own mistakes
    C. encourage cliques by given them information before giving it to other workers
    D. give adequate credit and praise when due

40. When a new employee reports to a custodian on his first day on the job, the custodian should 40.____
    A. extend a hearty welcome and make the new employee feel welcome
    B. have the man sit and wait for a while before seeing him so that the employee realizes how busy the custodian is
    C. warn him of stern disciplinary action if he is late or absent excessively
    D. tell him he probably will have difficulty doing the work so that he doesn't become overconfident

KEY (CORRECT ANSWERS)

1. A	11. A	21. D	31. C
2. D	12. D	22. C	32. A
3. C	13. A	23. C	33. D
4. B	14. D	24. B	34. C
5. B	15. C	25. C	35. C
6. C	16. C	26. C	36. D
7. A	17. D	27. C	37. D
8. C	18. B	28. A	38. C
9. D	19. D	29. A	39. D
10. B	20. A	30. C	40. A

EXAMINATION SECTION
TEST 1

DIRECTIONS: Each question or incomplete statement is followed by several suggested answers or completions. Select the one that BEST answers the question or completes the statement. *PRINT THE LETTER OF THE CORRECT ANSWER IN THE SPACE AT THE RIGHT.*

1. Which of the following chemicals is used to decrease the amount of oxygen in boiler water?
   A. Soda ash
   B. Sodium chloride
   C. Sodium sulfite
   D. Trisodium phosphate

2. The house tank in the basement of your school building has a pressure gauge 10 feet above the bottom of the tank.
   If a column of water weighs .434 pounds per square inch per foot and the pressure gauge reads 47 pounds per square inch, then the pressure on the booster pump at the base of the tank is MOST NEARLY, in pounds per square inch,
   A. 47   B. 52   C. 57.50   D. 51.25

3. Assume that a shipment of ammonia and bleach have just been delivered to your school and one of your cleaners asks to be instructed as to how the ammonia and bleach are to be stored.
   You should instruct him to store them
   A. *together*, because liquids are usually stored with other liquids
   B. *separately*, because shelf life is increased hen supplies are maintained in their own areas away from other supplies.
   C. *together*, because it is easier to keep an accurate inventory when supplies that are delivered together are stored together
   D. *separately*, because their containers could break and mix, creating a highly toxic gas

4. Of the following, which one is the MOST effective technique for motivating your employees?
   A. Regularly remind them that they receive a good salary and other benefits
   B. Publicly commend employees when they do good work
   C. Socialize with them during breaks and after working hours
   D. Overlook minor infractions and ignore rules that you disagree with

5. Which one of the following chemicals is used to melt ice and snow?
   A. Calcium chloride
   B. Soda ash
   C. Trisodium soot
   D. Sodium sulphite

6. Boiler *handholes* are used for
   A. climbing onto boilers
   B. lighting burners
   C. cleaning soot
   D. inspecting boilers

7. The true water level for a boiler in operation is determined by operating the
   A. pressure relief valve	B. blow-down valve
   C. aquastat	D. tri-cocks

8. There have been a number of illegal entries into your building during school hours, and the school principal asks you to padlock certain exit doors in the building to control such entry. You and the principal are both aware that there are laws prohibiting the padlocking of exit doors, but the principal maintains that closing off the doors in question would not impede easy exit from your building.
   You should
   A. have the doors locked as requested but also inform your supervisor as to your decision to do so and your reason for that decision
   B. refuse to have the doors locked and if the principal insists, refer him to your supervisor
   C. have the doors locked if, after looking into the matter, you determine that the remaining unlocked doors would be sufficient
   D. refuse to have the doors locked unless the principal overrules you and puts it in writing

9. You are in the boiler room when a steam line ruptures and the water in the gauge glass disappears.
   Of the following, your FIRST action should be to
   A. secure the fire
   B. shut down the vacuum pump
   C. add water to replace the escaping water
   D. secure the steam valve

10. The reading of the above gas meter diagram is
    A. 6929	B. 6939	C. 7929	D. 7939

11. Sight glasses are found
    A. on air compressors	B. in classroom doors
    C. in cross-corridor doors	D. on vision panels

12. Graphite is USUALLY used as a
    A. lubricant	B. cleaning compound
    C. sealant	D. boiler water additive

13. If you receive a yearly allowance of $52,000 for your school, what would MOST NEARLY be your bi-weekly allowance if you determined that figure based on a year of 365 days?
    A. $1,925.28	B. $1,961.30	C. $1,994.52	D. $2,000.00

14. Number 6 fuel oil is also known as
 A. crude oil B. bunker C oil C. gas oil D. kerosene

 14._____

15. Of the following CO_2 readings, which one indicates the LOWEST excess in the flue gas?
 A. 10.0% B. 12.0% C. 14.0% D. 15.0%

 15._____

16. A large section of a ceiling in an occupied classroom is hanging loosely.
 Of the following, which is the FIRST action you should take?
 A. Check for leaks in the floor above
 B. Have the ceiling replastered immediately
 C. Prepare a requisition for repair
 D. Have the room evacuated

 16._____

17. If you sometimes enforce rules with strong disciplinary action and at other times you enforce the same rules with mild disciplinary action, your practice is a
 A. *good* one, because it enables you to apply strict discipline to cleaners who accept it and to avoid confrontations with your more resistant workers
 B. *bad* one, because generally speaking strong disciplinary actions should be taken for infractions
 C. *good* one, because employees who are *kept guessing* about what supervisors are thinking are less likely to try to take advantage
 D. *bad* one, because discipline should be applied with consistency

 17._____

18. If one of your employee's gross salary is $38,000 a year and you must deduct 5.85% of that sum, you should deduct
 A. $2,223.00 B. $2,226.00 C. $2,235.00 D. $2,342.00

 18._____

19. The remote control switch of an oil-burning heating plant should be located
 A. at the boiler room exit door
 B. in the custodian's office
 C. between 2 and 5 feet from the boiler
 D. on the boiler at eye level

 19._____

20. Fire Department personnel, while making a routine inspection, issue violations for conditions existing in your building.
 Of the following, it is MOST appropriate for you to
 A. explain that because schools are city property, violations cannot be issued
 B. accept the violations as written and take follow-up action
 C. inform them that they must go through proper channels before issuing the violations
 D. volunteer information about other conditions possibly in violation

 20._____

21. Assume that your school building has three-phase wiring. Assume also that when you throw the start-up switch on a motor in your boiler room, the motor hums but does not turn.

 21._____

Of the following, the MOST likely cause for this is
- A. low voltage
- B. motor grounding
- C. low amperage
- D. a blown fuse

22. Two of your cleaners are entitled to retroactive pay of 18 cents per hour. One of the cleaners is to be paid retroactive money for 80 hours at straight time and 50 hours at time and a half. The other cleaner is entitled to 750 hours at straight time and 100 hours at time and a half.
What is the TOTAL amount of retroactive money to be paid to the two employees?
- A. $238.50
- B. $265.90
- C. $319.50
- D. $346.50

23. Of the following, the MOST likely cause of coal gas fumes is a(n)
- A. improperly banked fire
- B. high steam pressure
- C. improper water level
- D. heavy BTU content in coal being used

24. Boiler draft is measured in
- A. pounds per square inch
- B. degrees Fahrenheit
- C. inches of water
- D. cubic feet per minute

25. Of the following, which method should be used to check a CO_2 fire extinguisher?
- A. Discharge it
- B. Weigh it
- C. Read the gauge
- D. Shake it

26. A(n) _____ pump is used on a boiler system using number 6 oil
- A. transfer
- B. vacuum
- C. ejector
- D. sump

27. Your boiler water has a pH of 8. This means that the water is
- A. acidic
- B. neutral
- C. alkaline
- D. dirty

28. Assume that the high temperature on March 14 was 72°F and the low temperature was 52°F. The standard temperature for calculation of degree days is 65°F.
The number of degree days for March 4 is
- A. 3
- B. 7
- C. 13
- D. 20

29. Pig tails are commonly found on
- A. steam gauges
- B. water meters
- C. temperature recorders
- D. draft gauges

30. Your school principal complains to you that a workman making repairs to the windows in your building is making noise that is disrupting classroom instruction.

Of the following, the FIRST action you should take is to
- A. ignore the principal in the hope that the noise subsides
- B. tell the principal that there has to be a certain amount of noise when repair work is being done
- C. meet with the workman to discuss rescheduling the work in order to minimize disruption
- D. inform the workman's supervisor that you have received complaints and warn him that you will take further action if he fails to cooperate

31. *Checkerboard* floors are found in
    A. restrooms   B. boiler rooms   C. classrooms   D. lunchrooms

32. One of your cleaners has a gross bi-weekly salary of $736.94. If the federal tax deduction for that period is $127.92, the state tax deduction is $42.85, and the FICA is $61.02, the city decusion is $7.36, and the state disability is $.60, what is the cleaner's net pay?
    A. $239.75   B. $362.49   C. $497.19   D. $521.03

33. The operating automatic pressuretrol shuts down the burner when the
    A. oil pressure fluctuates due to high oil temperatures
    B. steam pressure fluctuates due to highly acidic feedwater
    C. oil pressure indicator arrow enters *red* or danger zone
    D. predetermined steam pressure setting is reached

34. The PROPER method for securing lighting globes is to tighten the thumb-screws
    A. hand tight
    B. snug and loosen ½ turn
    C. with pliers
    D. till they just support the globe

35. Persons running an adult program after school hours ask to use the school kitchen to set up a large coffee maker and utensils. Board of Education policy, however, prohibits such use of the kitchen by anyone other than school kitchen workers.
    Of the following, it would be MOST appropriate for you to
    A. explain that you are prohibited from doing so and offer an alternative
    B. allow them to use the kitchen if you know them to be responsible and they agree to clean up afterwards
    C. politely inform them that their request does not come under your jurisdiction
    D. allow them to use the kitchen and afterwards have your staff clean up

36. A damaged or loose spinner cup will cause
    A. high oil pressure
    B. loss of lubricant
    C. low oil pressure
    D. poor atomization of oil

37. If, during a pay period, one of your employees works 80 hours at the straight time rate of $8.40 per hour and works 16 hours at time and a half, the employee's gross pay for the period is
    A. $739.20   B. $806.40   C. $873.60   D. $1,008.00

38. The low water cut-off stops the
    A. boiler on low water
    B. sump pump on low water
    C. sump pump in emergencies
    D. water on low pressure

    38.____

39. Which of the following chemicals is used to increase alkalinity in feedwater?
    A. Calcium chloride
    B. Sodium chloride
    C. Sodium hydroxide
    D. Hydrogen peroxide

    39.____

40. Which of the following should be used to remove mildew from marble surfaces?
    A. Bleach
    B. Ammonia
    C. Scouring powder
    D. Trisodium

    40.____

KEY (CORRECT ANSWERS)

1.	C	11.	A	21.	D	31.	B
2.	B	12.	A	22.	C	32.	C
3.	D	13.	D	23.	A	33.	D
4.	B	14.	B	24.	C	34.	B
5.	A	15.	D	25.	B	35.	A
6.	D	16.	D	26.	A	36.	D
7.	D	17.	D	27.	C	37.	C
8.	B	18.	A	28.	A	38.	A
9.	A	19.	A	29.	A	39.	C
10.	A	20.	B	30.	C	40.	A

TEST 2

DIRECTIONS: Each question or incomplete statement is followed by several suggested answers or completions. Select the one that BEST answers the question or completes the statement. *PRINT THE LETTER OF THE CORRECT ANSWER IN THE SPACE AT THE RIGHT.*

1. You have been informed that your building allowance is going to be decreased as part of a city-wide economy drive.
   Of the following, which is the FIRST action you should take in this situation?
   A. Lay-off the worker with the least seniority.
   B. Reduce the amount and complexity of your work in order to absorb the decrease.
   C. Start using less expensive supplies and materials.
   D. Study your custodial operation to determine how best to minimize the effects of the cuts.

   1.____

2. The purpose of the vent line on an oil tank is to allow
   A. water in the oil to evaporate
   B. oil to drain if tank is overfilled
   C. for expansion of the oil as the oil temperature rises
   D. gases to escape into the atmosphere

   2.____

3. A reading of 45°C is indicated on your temperature recorder.
   This temperature, expressed in degrees Fahrenheit, is
   A. 77   B. 81   C. 113   D. 145

   3.____

4. A dark orange flame in a boiler indicates
   A. low draft
   B. that the refractory is damaged
   C. too much secondary air
   D. too much primary air

   4.____

5. *Metering* faucets
   A. are washerless
   B. have aerators
   C. shut off automatically
   D. vent air

   5.____

6. You are allowed $72,000 for the operation of your building. Of this amount, your salary is $32,000, your fireman's salary is $25,000, your cleaner earns $10,500, and compensation insurance will cost $750.00.
   After these monies are paid, how much will remain?
   A. $3,150   B. $3,750   C. $4,550   D. $4,570

   6.____

7. It has come to your attention that the police department has one of your cleaners under surveillance.
   Of the following, your action should be to
   A. tell the cleaner that he is under surveillance
   B. tell all your cleaners about the situation and warn them to avoid trouble
   C. terminate the cleaner under surveillance
   D. say nothing about the situation to the cleaner

   7.____

8. After you prepared a monthly payroll report and sent it to headquarters, you find that you made errors in the report.
   Of the following, it would be MOST important to
   A. do nothing since a payroll report would be thoroughly checked at headquarters
   B. make all the required changes on the copy you kept
   C. immediately resubmit the report to include the corrected information
   D. adjust the next month's figures to compensate for the error

8.____

9. Stay bolts are found in a boiler's
   A. brick setting
   B breeching
   C. fire doors
   D. shell

9.____

10. A *plumber's friend* is used to
    A. change washers
    B. stop leaks
    C. open corroded fittings
    D. clear stoppages

10.____

11. Ballasts are found in
    A. fluorescent fixtures
    B. plumbing fixtures
    C. boiler equalizers
    D. vacuum pumps

11.____

12. You hire a person as a cleaner on the recommendation of a friend of yours who is a custodian at another school.
    When dealing with the newly hired cleaner, it would be MOST appropriate for you to assign
    A. him to the same type of work as you would give to another cleaner with similar abilities
    B. less desirable work to him than you assign to other cleaners in order to avoid giving the impression that he will be receiving special treatment
    C. him work with no regard to his abilities since all workers should be treated the same
    D. him the most desirable work in order to maintain friendship with the custodian who recommended him and to encourage the newly hired cleaner to do good work

12.____

13. The size of a boiler tube is based on its
    A. inside diameter
    B. circumference
    C. outside diameter
    D. cross-sectional area

13.____

14. Of the following, the LEAST important consideration when preparing a work schedule is the
    A. number of employees on your staff
    B. type of work to be done
    C. age of the employees on your staff
    D. monies budgeted

14.____

15. A solenoid valve is also known as a _____ valve.
    A. magnetic oil
    B. thermo-electric
    C. hydraulic
    D. pressure

15.____

16. One of your employees earns $17.00 an hour and another employee earns $21.00 an hour. Last week, the employee making $17.00 an hour worked forty hours, and the employee earning $21.00 an hour worked forty-four hours. Assuming that all time in excess of forty hours a week is computed at time and a half, their combined gross pay for the week is
    A. $1,646.00   B. $1,680.00   C. $1,706.00   D. $1,752.00

17. Flame failure in a rotary up oil burner is detected by the
    A. vaporstat   B. aquastat
    C. low draft switch D. scanner

18. If the water coming from the faucets in your building is 95°C, it is
    A. warm   B. too hot   C. tepid   D. too cold

19. You are writing a memorandum to your supervisor concerning problems you have been having with certain boiler room equipment.
    Of the following, it would be MOST important for your memorandum to
    A. be long and include proper terminology to let your supervisor know you are technically competent and knowledgeable about proper boiler plant operation
    B. explain the problem clearly and to provide possible solutions
    C. explain the problem in such a way as to avoid giving the impression that the problems are your fault or that you did not do enough to minimize the effects
    D. be respectful in tone and grammatically correct

20. One of the classrooms in your building is often littered with paper, other trash, and in otherwise unacceptable condition at the end of the day.
    Of the following, it would be MOST appropriate for you to
    A. tell the children that they are to leave the room as clean at the end of the day as they find it in the morning
    B. speak to the principal about the room's condition in order to obtain her assistance to resolve the situation
    C. advise the teacher that you will instruct your cleaners not to clean the room unless he cooperates in keeping it clean
    D. regularly check the room to determine which of the children are responsible for its condition

21. One of your employees has a gross bi-weekly salary of $600 and a FICA deduction of 5%.
    His FICA deduction for a period of 4 weeks is
    A. $3   B. $6   C. $30   D. $60

22. A(n) _____ has a gauge glass.
    A. pressure gauge   B. inspection window
    C. condensate tank   D. transom

23. One standard square of roofing shingle will cover _____ square feet.
    A. 1   B. 10   C. 100   D. 144

24. _____ are NOT a part of low pressure boilers.
    A. Crown sheets   B. Impellers
    C. Weep holes   D. Stay rods

25. If one person is normally assigned to a facility for every 33,000 square feet and you have 82,000 square feet, your manpower requirement is
    A. 1   B. 1½   C. 2   D. 2½

26. Your cleaning crew's morale is very low because the school is often vandalized, making it very difficult for your workers to maintain the building properly.
    Of the following, it would be MOST appropriate for you to tell your crew
    A. that you are aware of the effort they put in even though the building does not reflect the work they do
    B. not to work so hard because their work is not appreciated and it is a losing battle
    C. that they get paid for their work and, therefore, there is no justification for their low morale
    D. not to concern themselves about vandalism since it is a social problem, not a custodial matter

27. Nematodes are
    A. weeds   B. elevator fuses
    C. electrical circuits D. lawn pests

28. A *supervisory* circuit is found in
    A. boiler controls   B. the principal's intercom
    C. hot water tanks   D. fire alarms

29. Braided packing is found in
    A. electrical insulation B. stuffing boxes
    C. wall insulation   D. junction boxes

30. The gas meter in your building reads 1234 on the 1st of the month and 1356 at the end of the month.
    If the meter has a multiplier of 60, how much gas was consumed for the month?
    A. 813.60   B. 4260   C. 7320   D. 81360

31. Which of the following is NOT used to control boiler water level? A
    A. condensate return pump   B. vacuum pump
    C. blow-down valve   D. feedwater regulator

32. A water-charged fire extinguisher should NOT be used on a(n) _____ fire.
    A. paper   B. oil   C. wood   D. trash

33. A *pope's head* is used to clean
    A. floors   B. boiler tubes   C. windows   D. sidewalks

34. The drain in your school yard is stopped up after each rainfall.
Which one of the following is the MOST appropriate action to take to correct this situation.
    A. Remove the strainer basket
    B. Schedule regular drain cleaning
    C. Blank off grating
    D. Have the drain *snaked* on an annual basis

35. Of the following, which is the LARGEST size of coal?
    A. Rice   B. Buckwheat   C. Pea   D. Walnut

36. To perform a low water cut-off test, you should
    A. shut off the water at the tempering valve
    B. open the bypass valve on the feedwater regulator
    C. shut down the water supply until the boiler shuts off
    D. open the pressure relief valve

37. A recently hired cleaner does not complete tasks within the time periods that you believe to be proper for his work.
Of the following, the FIRST action you should take is to
    A. warn him that his job may be in jeopardy if he does not improve
    B. avoid mentioning anything about his work for the first few weeks of his employment
    C. ask other employees to encourage him to work harder and faster
    D. observe him while he works to determine the reasons he takes so long to complete this work

38. This year, the fuel consumption at your school has significantly increased over last year's consumption even though the weather for both years has been quite similar. You are checking your heating system to determine the reason for the increase.
Which of the following is LEAST likely to be the reason for the higher consumption?
    A. Dirty fire tubes   B. Leaking steam traps
    C. High flue gas temperature   D. High steam temperature

39. A teacher tells you that one of your cleaners broke her classroom movie projector. She states that when she left the room at the end of the preceding school day, the cleaner was working in her room and the projector was operating fine. The next morning it wasn't working.
For this situation, you should FIRST
    A. accuse the cleaner of breaking it to test his reaction
    B. order the cleaner to talk to the teacher to get the matter resolved
    C. question the cleaner to find out what, if anything, he knows about the situation
    D. watch the cleaner for several days to see if he does anything to indicate guilt

40. Of the following, which is the MOST likely indication of soot build-up in boiler tubes? 40.____
    A. A high CO_2 reading
    B. A high furnace draft reading
    C. High boiler pressure
    D. High stack temperature

KEY (CORRECT ANSWERS)

1.	D	11.	A	21.	D	31.	B
2.	D	12.	A	22.	C	32.	B
3.	C	13.	C	23.	C	33.	C
4.	A	14.	C	24.	B	34.	B
5.	C	15.	A	25.	D	35.	C
6.	B	16.	A	26.	A	36.	C
7.	D	17.	D	27.	D	37.	D
8.	C	18.	B	28.	D	38.	D
9.	D	19.	B	29.	B	39.	C
10.	D	20.	B	30.	C	40.	D

EXAMINATION SECTION

TEST 1

DIRECTIONS: Each question or incomplete statement is followed by several suggested answers or completions. Select the one that BEST answers the question or completes the statement. *PRINT THE LETTER OF THE CORRECT ANSWER IN THE SPACE AT THE RIGHT.*

Questions 1-5.

DIRECTIONS: Column I lists cleaning jobs. Column II lists cleaning agents and devices. Select the PROPER cleansing agent from Column II for each job in Column I. Place the letter of the cleansing agent selected in the space at the right corresponding to the number of the cleaning job.

COLUMN I	COLUMN II	
1. Chewing gum	A. Muriatic acid	1._____
2. Ink stains	B. Broad bladed knife	2._____
3. Fingermarks on glass	C. Kerosene	3._____
4. Rust stains on porcelain	D. Oxalic acid	4._____
5. Hardened dirt on porcelain	E. Lye	5._____
	F. Linseed oil	

6. When the bristles of a floor brush have worn short, the brush should be 6._____
   A. thrown away and the handles saved
   B. saved and the brush used on rough cement floors
   C. saved and used for high dusting in classrooms
   D. saved and used for the weekly scrubbing of linoleum floors

7. Feather dusters should NOT be used because they 7._____
   A. take more time to use than other dusters
   B. cannot be cleaned
   C. do not take up the dust but merely move it from one place to another
   D. do not stir up the dust and streak the furniture with dust rails

8. Floors that are usually NOT waxed are those made of 8._____
   A. pine wood   B. mastic tile   C. rubber tile   D. terrazzo

9. For sweeping under radiators and other inaccessible places, the MOST appropriate tool is the 9._____
   A. counter brush
   B. dry mop
   C. feather duster
   D. 16" floor brush

10. A cleansing agent that should NOT be used in the cleaning of windows is
    A. water containing fine pumice
    B. water containing a small amount of ammonia
    C. water containing a little kerosene
    D. a paste cleanser made from water and cleaning powder

11. The BEST way to dust desks is to use a
    A. circular motion with soft dry cloth that has been washed
    B. damp cloth, taking care not to disturb papers on the desk
    C. soft cloth, moistened with oil, using a back and forth motion
    D. back and forth motion with a soft dry cloth

12. Trisodium phosphate is a substance BEST used in
    A. washing kalsomined walls
    B. polishing of brass
    C. washing mastic tile floors
    D. clearing stoppages

13. Treated linoleum is PROPERLY cleaned by daily
    A. dusting with a treated mop
    B. sweeping with a floor brush
    C. mopping with a weak soap solution
    D. mopping after removal of dust with a floor brush

14. Of the following, the MOST proper use of chamois skin is
    A. drying of window glass after washing
    B. washing of window glass
    C. polishing of metal fixtures
    D. drying toilet bowls after washing

15. A squeegee is a tool which is used in
    A. cleaning stoppages in waste lines
    B. the central vacuum cleaning system
    C. cleaning inside boiler surfaces
    D. drying windows after washing

16. Concrete and cement floors are usually painted a battleship gray color. The MOST important reason for painting the floor is
    A. to improve the appearance of the floor
    B. the paint prevents the absorption of too much water when the floor is mopped
    C. the paint makes the floor safer and less slippery
    D. the concrete becomes harder and will not settle

17. A resin-base floor finish USUALLY
    A. gives the highest lustre of all floor finishes
    B. should be applied in one heavy coat
    C. provides a slip-resistant surface
    D. should not be used on asphalt tile

18. The one of the following cleaning operations on soft floors that generally requires MOST NEARLY the same amount of time per 1,000 square feet as damp mopping is
    A. applying a thin coat of wax
    B. sweeping
    C. dust mopping
    D. wet mopping

18.____

19. Of the following cleaning jobs, the one that should be allowed the MOST time to complete a 1,000 square foot area is
    A. vacuuming carpets
    B. washing painted walls
    C. stripping and waxing soft floors
    D. machine-scrubbing hard floors

19.____

20. When instructing your staff in the use of sodium silicate, you should tell them that it is MOST commonly used to
    A. seal concrete floors
    B. condition leather
    C. treat boiler water
    D. neutralize acid wastes

20.____

21. Cleaners should be instructed that dust mopping is LEAST appropriate for removing light soil from _____ floors.
    A. terrazzo
    B. unsealed concrete
    C. resin-finished soft
    D. sealed wood

21.____

22. Of the following, the substance that should be recommended for polishing hardwood furniture is
    A. lemon oil polish
    B. neatsfoot oil
    C. paste wax
    D. water-emulsion wax

22.____

23. The use of concentrated acid to remove stains from ceramic tile bathroom floors USUALLY results in making the surface
    A. pitted and porous
    B. clean and shiny
    C. harder and glossier
    D. waterproof

23.____

24. Asphalt tile floors should be protected by coating with
    A. hard-milled soap
    B. water-emulsion wax
    C. sodium metaphosphate
    D. varnish

24.____

25. Of the following, the BEST way to economize on cleaning tools and materials is to
    A. train the cleaners to use them properly
    B. order at least a three-year supply of every item in order to avoid annual price increases
    C. attach a price sticker to every item so that the people using them will realize their high cost
    D. delay ordering material for three months at the beginning of each year to be sure that the old material is used to the fullest extent

25.____

KEY (CORRECT ANSWERS)

1.	B	11.	D
2.	D	12.	C
3.	C	13.	A
4.	A	14.	A
5.	C	15.	D
6.	B	16.	B
7.	C	17.	C
8.	D	18.	A
9.	A	19.	C
10.	A	20.	A

21. B
22. C
23. A
24. B
25. A

TEST 2

DIRECTIONS: Each question or incomplete statement is followed by several suggested answers or completions. Select the one that BEST answers the question or completes the statement. *PRINT THE LETTER OF THE CORRECT ANSWER IN THE SPACE AT THE RIGHT.*

1. Of the following office cleaning jobs performed during the year, the one which should be done MOST frequently is
   A. cleaning the fluorescent lights
   B. dusting the Venetian blinds
   C. cleaning the bookcase glass
   D. carpetsweeping the rug

   1._____

2. The BEST polishing agent to use on wood furniture is
   A. pumice
   B. paste wax
   C. water emulsion wax
   D. neatsfoot oil

   2._____

3. Lemon oil polish is used BEST to polish
   A. exterior bronze
   B. marble walls
   C. leather seats
   D. lacquered metal

   3._____

4. Cleaning with trisodium phosphate is MOST likely to damage
   A. toilet bowls
   B. drain pipes
   C. polished marble floors
   D. rubber tile floors

   4._____

5. Of the following cleaning agents, the one which should NOT be used to remove stains from urinals is
   A. caustic lye   B. detergent   C. oxalic acid   D. muriatic acid

   5._____

6. The one of the following cleaners which GENERALLY contains an abrasive is
   A. caustic lye
   B. trisodium phosphate
   C. scouring powder
   D. ammonia

   6._____

7. The instructions on a box of cleaning powder say: *Mix one pound of cleaning powder in four gallons of water.*
   According to these instructions, how many ounces of cleaning powder should be mixed in one gallon of water?
   A. 4   B. 8   C. 12   D. 16

   7._____

8. In accordance with recommended practice, a dust mop, when not being used, should be stored
   A. hanging, handle end down
   B. hanging, handle end up
   C. standing on the floor, handle end down
   D. standing on the floor, handle end up

   8._____

9. The two types of floors found in public buildings are classified as hard floors and soft floors.
An example of a hard floor is one made of
A. linoleum B. cork C. ceramic tile D. asphalt tile

10. A squeegee is a tool that is MAINLY used to clean
A. painted walls
B. radiator covers
C. window glass
D. ceramic tile floors

11. The BEST way to determine whether a cleaner is doing his work well is by
A. observing the cleaner at work for several hours
B. asking the cleaner questions about his work
C. asking other cleaners to rate his work
D. inspecting the cleanliness of the spaces assigned to the cleaner

12. The PRIMARY purpose of using a disinfectant material is to
A. kill germs
B. destroy odors
C. remove stains
D. kill insects

13. Windows should be washed by using a solution of warm water mixed with
A. chlorine bleach
B. kerosene
C. ammonia
D. soft soap

14. Of the following, the MOST effective way to reduce waste of cleaning tools is to
A. keep careful records of how often tools are issued
B. require that the old tool be returned before issuing a new one
C. require that all tools be used for a fixed number of hours before replacing them
D. train the cleaners to use the tools properly

15. The number of square feet of unobstructed corridor floor space that a cleaner should sweep in an hour is MOST NEARLY
A. 1200 B. 2400 C. 4000 D. 6000

16. Sweeping compound is used on concrete floors MAINLY to
A. polish the floor
B. keep the dust down
C. soften the encrusted dirt
D. provide a non-slip surface

17. The BEST attachment to use on an electric scrubbing machine when stripping waxed resilient flooring is a
A. nylon disk
B. soft brush
C. steel wool pad
D. pumice wheel

18. A counter brush is BEST suited to cleaning
A. water cooler drains
B. radiators
C. light fixtures
D. lavatory fixtures

19. In high dusting of walls and ceilings, the CORRECT procedure is to
    A. begin with lower walls and process up to the ceiling
    B. remove pictures and window shades only if they are dusty
    C. clean the windows thoroughly before dusting any other part of the room
    D. begin with the ceiling, then dust the walls

    19.____

20. When cleaning a room, the cleaner should
    A. dust desks before sweeping
    B. dust desks after sweeping
    C. open windows wide during the desk dusting process
    D. begin dusting at rows most distant from entrance door

    20.____

21. Too much water on asphalt tile is objectionable MAINLY because the tile
    A. will tend to become discolored or spotted
    B. may be loosened from the floor
    C. will be softened and made uneven
    D. colors will tend to run

    21.____

22. To reduce the slip hazard resulting from waxing linoleum, the MOST practical of the following methods is
    A. apply the wax in one heavy coat
    B. apply the wax after varnishing the linoleum
    C. buff the wax surface thoroughly
    D. apply the wax in several thin coats

    22.____

23. Assume that the water emulsion wax needed for routine waxing in your building is 15 gallons per month. This wax is supplied in 55-gallon drums.
    To cover your needs for a year, the MINIMUM number of drums you would have to request is
    A. two   B. three   C. four   D. six

    23.____

24. In washing down the walls, the correct procedure is to start at the bottom of the wall and work to the top.
    The MOST important reason for this is:
    A. Dirt streaking will tend to be avoided or easily removed
    B. Less cleansing agent will be required
    C. Rinse water will not be required
    D. The time for cleaning the wall is less than if washing at the top of the wall

    24.____

25. In mopping a wood floor, the cleaner should
    A. mop against the grain of the wood wherever possible
    B. mop as large an area as possible at one time
    C. wet the floor before mopping with a cleaning agent
    D. mop only aisles and clear areas and use a scrub brush under desks and chairs

    25.____

KEY (CORRECT ANSWERS)

1.	D	11.	D
2.	B	12.	A
3.	A	13.	C
4.	C	14.	D
5.	D	15.	D
6.	C	16.	B
7.	A	17.	A
8.	B	18.	B
9.	C	19.	D
10.	C	20.	B

21. B
22. D
23. C
24. A
25. C

TEST 3

DIRECTIONS: Each question or incomplete statement is followed by several suggested answers or completions. Select the one that BEST answers the question or completes the statement. *PRINT THE LETTER OF THE CORRECT ANSWER IN THE SPACE AT THE RIGHT.*

1. The MAIN reason for using a sweeping compound is to
   A. spot-finish waxed surfaces
   B. retard dust when sweeping floors
   C. loosen accumulations of grease
   D. remove paint spots from the flooring

   1.____

2. The one of the following cleaning agents which is recommended for use on marble floors is
   A. an acid cleaner
   B. a soft soap
   C. trisodium phosphate
   D. a neutral liquid detergent

   2.____

3. A cleaning solution of one cup of soap chips dissolved in a pail of warm water can be used to wash
   A. painted walls
   B. rubber tile
   C. marble walls
   D. terrazzo floors

   3.____

4. Sodium fluoride is a
   A. pesticide   B. disinfectant   C. detergent   D. paint thinner

   4.____

5. Scratches or burns in linoleum, rubber tile, or cork floors should be removed by rubbing with
   A. crocus cloth
   B. fine steel wool
   C. sandpaper
   D. emery cloth

   5.____

6. A room 12 feet wide by 25 feet long has a floor area of _____ square feet.
   A. 37   B. 200   C. 300   D. 400

   6.____

7. A cleaning solution should be applied to a painted wall using a
   A. wool rag   B. brush   C. sponge   D. squeegee

   7.____

8. When scrubbing a wooden floor, it is ADVISABLE to
   A. flood the surface with the cleaning solution in order to float the dirt out of all cracks and crevices
   B. hose off the loosened dirt before starting the scrubbing operation
   C. pick up the cleaning solution as soon as possible
   D. mix a mild acid with the cleaning solution in order to clean the surface quickly

   8.____

9. How many hours will it take a worker to sweep a floor space of 2800 square feet if he sweeps at the pace of 800 square feet per hour?
   A. 8   B. 6½   C. 3½   D. 2½

   9.____

10. One gallon of water contains
    A. 2 quarts   B. 4 quarts   C. 2 pints   D. 4 pints

11. A standard cleaning solution is prepared by mixing 4 ounces of detergent powder in 2 gallons of water.
    The number of ounces of detergent powder needed for the same strength solution in 5 gallons of water is
    A. 4   B. 6   C. 8   D. 10

12. The principal reason why soap should NOT be used in cleaning windows is
    A. it causes loosening of the putty
    B. it may cause rotting of the wood frames
    C. a film is left on the window, requiring additional rinsing
    D. frequent use of soap will cause the glass to become permanently clouded

13. When a window pane is broken, the FIRST step the custodian takes is to
    A. remove broken glass from floors and the window sill
    B. determine the cause
    C. remove the putty with a putty knife
    D. prepare a piece of glass to replace the broken pane

14. Your instructions to a cleaner about the proper sweeping of offices should include the following instruction:
    A. Do not move chairs and wastebaskets from their places when sweeping
    B. Place chairs and baskets on the desks to get them out of the way
    C. Set aside the loose small furniture and chairs in an orderly manner when sweeping office floors
    D. Move the desks and chairs to the side of the room close to the wall in order to sweep properly

15. To remove dirt accumulations after the completion of the sweeping task, brushes should be
    A. tapped on the floor in the normal sweeping position
    B. struck on the floor against the side of the block
    C. struck on the floor against the end of the block
    D. turned upside down and the handle tapped on the floor

16. To sweep rough cement floors in a basement, the BEST tool to use is a
    A. deck brush   B. new 30" floor brush
    C. corn broom   D. treated mop

17. When a floor is scrubbed, it is NOT correct to
    A. use a steady, even rotary motion
    B. rinse the floor with clean hot water
    C. have the mop strokes follow the boards when drying the floor
    D. wet the floor first by pouring several bucketsful of water on it

18. Flushing with a hose is MOST appropriate as a method of cleaning
    A. terrazzo floors of corridors
    B. untreated wood floors
    C. linoleum floors where not in frequent use
    D. cement floors

19. Improper use of a carbon dioxide type portable fire extinguisher may cause injury to the operator because
    A. handling the nozzle during discharge can cause frostbite to the skin
    B. carbon dioxide is highly poisonous if breathed into the lungs
    C. use of carbon dioxide on an oil fire can cause a chemical explosion
    D. the powdery residue left by the discharge is highly caustic to the skin

20. When using a portable single ladder with ten rungs, the GREATEST number of rungs that a cleaner should climb up is
    A. 7 B. 8 C. 9 D. 10

21. Of the following types of portable fire extinguishers, the one which should be used to control a fire in or around live electrical equipment is the _____ type.
    A. foam
    B. soda acid
    C. carbon dioxide
    D. gas cartridge water

22. The MOST frequent cause of accidental injuries to workers on the job is
    A. unsafe working practices of employees
    B. poor design of buildings and working areas
    C. lack of warning signs in hazardous work areas
    D. lack of adequate safety guards on equipment and machinery

23. Of the following, the MOST important purpose of preparing an accident report on an injury to a cleaner is to help
    A. collect statistics on different types of accidents
    B. calm the feelings of the injured cleaner
    C. prevent similar accidents in the future
    D. prove that the cleaner was at fault

24. The one of the following types of locks that is used on emergency exit doors is the
    A. panic B. dead C. cinch D. toggle

25. The one of the following types of locks that USUALLY contains both a live volt and a dead bolt is a _____ lock.
    A. mortise
    B. double-hung window
    C. loose pin butt
    D. window frame

KEY (CORRECT ANSWERS)

1.	B	11.	D
2.	D	12.	C
3.	A	13.	A
4.	A	14.	C
5.	B	15.	A
6.	C	16.	C
7.	C	17.	D
8.	C	18.	D
9.	C	19.	A
10.	B	20.	B

21. C
22. A
23. C
24. A
25. A

———

EXAMINATION SECTION
TEST 1

DIRECTIONS: Each question or incomplete statement is followed by several suggested answers or completions. Select the one that BEST answers the question or completes the statement. *PRINT THE LETTER OF THE CORRECT ANSWER IN THE SPACE AT THE RIGHT.*

Questions 1-5.

DIRECTIONS: For Questions 1 through 5, inclusive, Column I lists frequently used construction terms. Column II lists some of the building trades. For each item listed in Column I, enter in the appropriate space at the right the capital letter in front of the trade listed in Column II that is MOST closely associated with the item. Each trade may be used more than once or not at all.

COLUMN I	COLUMN II
1. Bed	A. Plumbing
2. Wiping	B. Plastering
3. Brown	C. Carpentry
4. Key	D. Masonry
5. Bridging	E. Painting
	F. Steelwork
	G. Roofing

1.____
2.____
3.____
4.____
5.____

6. A *cricket* would be found

    A. on a roof
    B. at a structural steel connection
    C. supporting reinforcing steel
    D. over a window

6.____

7. *Cutting in* is done when

    A. trimming a stud to size
    B. fitting a bat in a brick wall
    C. painting in tight corners
    D. trimming tallow for a wiped joint

7.____

8. *Corbeling* results in

    A. strengthening a concrete column
    B. waterproofing a foundation wall
    C. anchoring a steel girder to a bearing wall
    D. increasing the thickness of a brick wall

8.____

9. Solder used for copper gutters is MOST frequently

   A. 30-70   B. 40-60   C. 50-50   D. 60-40

10. A jack rafter runs from

    A. plate to ridge
    B. hip to ridge
    C. plate to hip
    D. plate to plate

11. The one of the following items that is LEAST related to the others is

    A. sill   B. joist   C. sole   D. newel

12. A *fire cut* is made on

    A. timber posts
    B. rafters
    C. floor joists
    D. lathing

13. The one of the following items that is LEAST related to the others is

    A. joist hanger
    B. pintle
    C. bridle iron
    D. stirrup

14. The PROPER order of nailing sub-flooring and bridging is

    A. top of bridging, bottom of bridging, sub-flooring
    B. bottom of bridging, sub-flooring, top of bridging
    C. top of bridging, sub-flooring, bottom of bridging
    D. bottom of bridging, top of bridging, sub-flooring

15. Sleepers would be found in

    A. walls   B. doors   C. footings   D. floors

16. The one of the following woods that is MOST commonly used for finish flooring is

    A. hemlock   B. cypress   C. larch   D. oak

17. Spacing of studs in a stud partition is MOST frequently _____ " o.c.

    A. 12   B. 14   C. 16   D. 18

18. A hollow masonry wall should be used in preference to a solid masonry wall when the characteristic MOST desired is

    A. insulation
    B. strength
    C. beauty
    D. durability

19. The arrangement of headers and stretchers in brickwork is known as the

    A. bond   B. stringer   C. lacing   D. stile

20. Of the following, the reason that is LEAST likely to justify pointing brickwork is that pointing _____ the wall.

    A. improves the appearance of
    B. helps prevent cracking of
    C. increases the useful life of
    D. helps waterproof

21. The purpose of flashing is to 21.____

    A. keep water out B. speed the set of mortar
    C. anchor a cornice D. cover exposed joists

22. The one of the following classes of wall that would LEAST likely be the outside wall of a building is a 22.____

    A. spandrel B. fire C. curtain D. parapet

23. Lime is added to mortar USUALLY to 23.____

    A. increase the strength of the mortar
    B. make the mortar water resistant
    C. make it easier to apply the mortar
    D. improve the appearance of the mortar joint

24. Efflorescence on the face of a brick wall is BEST removed by scrubbing with a solution of 24.____

    A. muriatic acid B. sodium silicate
    C. oxalic acid D. calcium oxide

25. The one of the following that is NOT a defect in painting is 25.____

    A. chalking B. checking
    C. alligatoring D. waning

26. The one of the following ingredients of a paint that would be called the *vehicle* is 26.____

    A. white lead B. turpentine
    C. linseed oil D. pigment

27. The one of the following that is used as a rust preventative in the prime coat for painting steel is 27.____

    A. aluminum B. red lead
    C. titanium dioxide D. carbon black

28. *Boxing*, with reference to paint, means 28.____

    A. thinning B. mixing C. spreading D. drying

29. When painting new wood, filling of nail holes and cracks with putty should be done 29.____

    A. 24 hours before priming
    B. immediately before priming
    C. after priming and before the second coat
    D. after the second coat and before the finish coat

30. The one of the following that is the size of a reinforcing rod MOST commonly used in reinforced concrete construction is 30.____

    A. 1 3/4" ϕ B. 18 gauge C. #9 D. 2 ST3

31. Honeycombing in concrete is USUALLY caused by 31.____

    A. too plastic a mix B. high fall of concrete
    C. mixing too long D. inadequate vibration

32. A concrete mix is indicated as 1:2:3 1/2 mix. The number 2 refers to the proportion by volume of

   A. water   B. cement   C. gravel   D. sand

33. Specifications for concrete mixes frequently call for the use of dry sand. The reason for this is that the additional water in wet sand will

   A. make it more difficult to place the concrete
   B. decrease the strength of the concrete
   C. cause the sand and stone to segregate
   D. increase the cost of waterproofing

34. Curing of concrete serves PRIMARILY to

   A. prevent freezing of the concrete
   B. permit early removal of forms
   C. delay setting of the concrete
   D. prevent evaporation of moisture

35. The MAIN reason that forms for concrete work are oiled is to

   A. *permit* easy removal of forms
   B. *prevent* rust marks on the concrete
   C. *prevent* bleeding of water
   D. *permit* easier vibration of the concrete

36. The one of the following terms that is LEAST related to the others is

   A. 5-ply   B. mastic
   C. vapor barrier   D. flashing

37. Before quicklime can be used for plaster, it must be

   A. slaked   B. burned   C. floated   D. glazed

38. When a hard plaster is required, as in halls, the one of the following that would MOST likely be used is

   A. lime   B. Keene's cement
   C. stucco   D. marbling

39. To give plaster a hard finish, hydrated lime is mixed with

   A. white cement   B. linseed oil putty
   C. white lead   D. plaster of paris

40. The purpose of a ground in plaster work is to

   A. provide a key for the plaster
   B. help the plasterer make an even wall
   C. prevent the plasterer's scaffold from slipping
   D. hold the loose plaster before it is placed

41. When a lightweight plaster is required, the one of the following fine aggregates that is MOST likely to be used is

    A. cinders
    B. sand
    C. talc
    D. vermiculite

42. Of the following fireproofing materials, the one which would be MOST frequently used to fireproof steel columns in a fireproof building is

    A. sheet rock
    B. vermiculite plaster
    C. brick
    D. rock lath

43. The one of the following items that is LEAST related to the others is

    A. rock wool
    B. wall board
    C. sheet rock
    D. rock lath

44. The first layer of plaster placed in a 3-coat plaster job is called the _____ coat.

    A. brown   B. scratch   C. hard   D. white

45. The one of the following symbols that represents a steel section which is MOST similar in appearance to a W section is

    A. U   B. L   C. I   D. Z

46. A plate used to connect two steel angles in a roof truss is known as a(n)

    A. angle iron
    B. gusset plate
    C. bearing plate
    D. tie bar

47. Steel beams are COMMONLY anchored to brick walls by

    A. government anchors
    B. tie rods
    C. eye bars
    D. anchor bolts

48. Rivet holes are lined up with a

    A. set screw
    B. ginnywink
    C. drift pin
    D. trivet

49. A sewer that carries BOTH storm water and sewage is called a _____ sewer.

    A. sanitary   B. flush   C. combined   D. mixed

50. A fresh air inlet for a house drainage system would be connected to the system

    A. just ahead of the house trap
    B. at each horizontal branch line
    C. at the top of the stack through the roof
    D. at the trap of each water closet

KEY (CORRECT ANSWERS)

1. D	11. D	21. A	31. D	41. D
2. A	12. C	22. B	32. D	42. B
3. B	13. B	23. C	33. B	43. A
4. B	14. C	24. A	34. D	44. B
5. C	15. D	25. D	35. A	45. C
6. A	16. D	26. C	36. C	46. B
7. C	17. C	27. B	37. A	47. A
8. D	18. A	28. B	38. B	48. C
9. C	19. A	29. C	39. D	49. C
10. C	20. B	30. C	40. B	50. A

TEST 2

DIRECTIONS: Each question or incomplete statement is followed by several suggested answers or completions. Select the one that BEST answers the question or completes the statement. *PRINT THE LETTER OF THE CORRECT ANSWER IN THE SPACE AT THE RIGHT.*

Questions 1-5.

DIRECTIONS: Column I consists of a list of trades, and Column II lists tools used in those trades. In the space at the right, opposite the number of the trade in Column I, write the letter preceding the tool of the trade in Column II.

COLUMN I		COLUMN II	
1.	Carpenter	A.	Mop
2.	Plumber	B.	Hawk
3.	Plasterer	C.	Miter box
4.	Bricklayer	D.	Shave-hook
5.	Roofer	E.	Jointing tool

1.____
2.____
3.____
4.____
5.____

Questions 6-7.

DIRECTIONS: Questions 6 and 7 refer to the mortar joints shown below.

6. The mortar joint MOST frequently used on common brickwork is 6.____
   A. 1   B. 2   C. 3   D. 4

7. The mortar joint which would NOT usually be made unless an outside scaffold was used is 7.____
   A. 1   B. 2   C. 3   D. 4

8. A rectangular yard is 50'0" long by 8'6" wide. 8.____
   The area of the yard is, in square feet,
   A. 420.0   B. 422.5   C. 425.0   D. 427.5

87

9. A rectangular court is 23'0" long by 9'6" wide.
   The length of the diagonal is MOST NEARLY

   A. 24'8"   B. 24'10"   C. 25'2"   D. 25'6"

10. Concrete weighs 150 pounds per cubic foot.
    A slab of concrete 6'0" long by 3'6" wide by 1'4" thick weighs MOST NEARLY _____ pounds.

    A. 4150   B. 4200   C. 4250   D. 4300

11. A building 32'0" by 65'0" occupies a lot 60'0" by 110'0". The ratio of building area to lot area is MOST NEARLY

    A. 0.32   B. 0.33   C. 0.34   D. 0.35

12. When painting wood, puttying of nail holes and cracks is done

    A. before any painting is started
    B. after the priming coat is applied
    C. after the finish coat is applied
    D. at any stage in the painting

13. The process of pouring paint from one container to another in order to mix it is known as

    A. bleeding   B. boxing   C. cutting   D. stirring

14. Paint is *thinned* with

    A. linseed oil   B. turpentine
    C. varnish   D. gasoline

15. A wood screw which can be tightened by a wrench is known as a _____ screw.

    A. lag   B. Philips   C. carriage   D. monkey

16. To permit easy removal of forms from concrete, the inside surfaces of the forms are often coated with

    A. paint   B. oil   C. water   D. asphalt

17. Sixteen pieces of 2 x 4 lumber, each 10'6" long, contain a total of _____ FBM.

    A. 110   B. 111   C. 112   D. 113

18. The consistency of concrete is measured with a

    A. Vicat needle   B. slump cone
    C. hook gage   D. bourdon gage

19. End-matched lumber would MOST likely be used for

    A. sheathing   B. roofing   C. flooring   D. siding

20. A post or shore is to be placed midway between columns to support the formwork for a reinforced concrete girder. The post should be cut

    A. short, so that wedging is required
    B. to exact length

C. long, so that it will have to be driven into place
D. in two pieces, to permit jackknifing into place

21. Batter boards are set by a

   A. mason   B. plumber   C. roofer   D. surveyor

22. Of the following terms, all of which refer to tools, the one which is LEAST related to the others is

   A. back   B. box-end   C. cross-cut   D. rip

23. Of the following tools, the one which is LEAST like the others is

   A. brace and bit
   B. draw-knife
   C. plans
   D. spoke-shave

24. When wood splits easily, it is advisable to drill a hole for each nail. The hole for the nail should be _____ the nail.

   A. larger in diameter than
   B. smaller in diameter than
   C. exactly the same diameter as
   D. less than one-quarter the length of

25. The length of a 10-penny nail, in inches, is

   A. $2\frac{1}{2}$ B. 3   C. $3\frac{1}{2}$ D. 4

26. The decimal equivalent of 31/64 of an inch is MOST NEARLY

   A. 0.45   B. 0.46   C. 0.47   D. 0.48

27. Of the following, the one which is BEST classified as an abrasive is

   A. a saw   B. a chisel   C. graphite   D. sandpaper

28. Of the following construction materials, the one which would MOST likely be stored directly on the ground is

   A. brick   B. cement   C. steel   D. wood

29. The strength of brick walls is based upon the type of mortar used. The relative strength of the various types of mortar, in descending order, is

   A. cement, lime, cement-lime
   B. lime, cement-lime, cement
   C. cement-lime, cement, lime
   D. cement, cement-lime, lime

30. Coating reinforcing rods with oil before placing them in the forms is

   A. *good* practice, because it prevents rusting
   B. *poor* practice, because it makes the rods difficult to handle
   C. *good* practice if the forms are oiled
   D. *poor* practice, because it destroys the bond between the concrete and the rods

31. If the mixing plant should break down after one-half the concrete has been mixed for a floor, the BEST thing to do would be to

    A. take the concrete out of the forms and throw it away
    B. spread the available concrete evenly over the floor area
    C. block off one-half of the floor area and place the available concrete in the blocked-off area
    D. keep mixing the concrete in the forms with shovels until the plant is repaired

32. Splicing of reinforcing bars is accomplished by

    A. using wire ties
    B. underlapping the bars
    C. hooking the bars
    D. using metal clips

33. A sanitary sewer carries

    A. storm water only
    B. sewage only
    C. sewage and storm water
    D. the discharge from a sewage plant

34. A neat line

    A. is the result of good workmanship
    B. is used in concrete construction only
    C. defines an outer limit of a structure
    D. defines an outer limit of excavation for a structure

35. Continued trowelling of a cement-finish floor for a building is

    A. *good* practice, because it provides a smooth floor
    B. *poor* practice, because it produces a slippery floor
    C. *poor* practice, because it brings the fines to the surface
    D. *good* practice, because it insures proper mixing of the cement finish

36. In reinforced concrete form work, a beveled chamfer strip is used to

    A. reinforce the outside of the forms
    B. reinforce the inside of the forms
    C. seal leaks in the forms
    D. do none of the foregoing

37. Cracks in lumber due to contraction along annual rings are known as

    A. checks
    B. wanes
    C. pitch pockets
    D. dry rot

38. Honeycombing is MOST likely to occur in construction involving

    A. steel
    B. concrete
    C. wood
    D. masonry

39. Floor beams are sometimes crowned to

    A. provide arch action
    B. eliminate deflection
    C. strengthen the floor
    D. provide a more nearly level floor than would be provided by straight beams

40. In brickwork, a rowlock course consists of 40.____

    A. headers
    B. stretchers
    C. bricks laid on edge
    D. bricks laid so that the longest dimension is vertical

41. The term *bond,* as used in bricklaying, refers to 41.____

    A. structure only
    B. pattern only
    C. structure and pattern
    D. color and finish of individual bricks

42. Concrete is a mixture of cement, 42.____

    A. fine aggregate, coarse aggregate, and water
    B. sand, and water
    C. stone, and water
    D. sand, and stone

43. Consistency, when used in connection with concrete, refers to the 43.____

    A. seven-day strength
    B. twenty-eight day strength
    C. initial set before forms are removed
    D. plasticity of freshly mixed concrete

44. Brick may be used for the facing material in both faced walls and veneered walls. 44.____
    The distinction between the two types of walls relates to

    A. bonding or lack of bonding between facing and backing
    B. type of material in facing and backing
    C. relative thickness of facing and backing
    D. the type of mortar used

45. A plaster *key* is NOT formed on _____ lath. 45.____

    A. wood   B. metal
    C. expanded metal   D. gypsum

46. Of the following, the BEST tool to use to make a hole in a coping stone is a 46.____

    A. star drill   B. coping saw
    C. pneumatic grinder   D. diamond wheel dresser

47. Roughing refers to work performed by a 47.____

    A. carpenter   B. bricklayer
    C. plumber   D. roofer

48. A post supporting a handrail is known as a 48.____

    A. tread   B. riser   C. newel   D. bevel

49. The live load on a floor is 40 pounds per square foot. The floor joists are on a 14'0" span and are spaced 2'6" on centers.
The maximum live load carried by a joist, in pounds, is MOST NEARLY

   A. 700 B. 933 C. 1167 D. 1400

50. Of the following terms, the one LEAST related to the others is

   A. ground
   B. purlin
   C. rafter
   D. ridge board

KEY (CORRECT ANSWERS)

1. C	11. A	21. D	31. C	41. C
2. D	12. B	22. B	32. A	42. A
3. B	13. B	23. A	33. B	43. D
4. E	14. B	24. B	34. C	44. A
5. A	15. A	25. B	35. C	45. D
6. C	16. B	26. D	36. D	46. A
7. A	17. C	27. D	37. A	47. C
8. C	18. B	28. A	38. B	48. C
9. B	19. C	29. D	39. D	49. D
10. B	20. A	30. D	40. C	50. A

EXAMINATION SECTION
TEST 1

DIRECTIONS: Each question or incomplete statement is followed by several suggested answers or completions. Select the one that BEST answers the question or completes the statement. *PRINT THE LETTER OF THE CORRECT ANSWER IN THE SPACE AT THE RIGHT.*

1. The BEST course of action to take to settle a job-related dispute that has arisen among two of your employees is to

    A. bring them both together, listen to their arguments, and then make a decision
    B. tell the two employees individually to settle their dispute
    C. tell both employees to submit their dispute in writing to you and then make a decision
    D. listen to the argument of each one separately and then make a decision

2. A custodian accidentally discovers a bottle of whiskey in a staff member's desk. The BEST procedure for the custodian to follow is to

    A. verbally reprimand him and prefer departmental charges
    B. inform him that whiskey is not allowed in school buildings
    C. call a meeting of all the employees and tell them what you found
    D. do nothing as you do not want to embarrass the person

3. A new employee under your supervision constantly reports late for work. The one of the following actions you should take FIRST is to

    A. admonish him in front of the other employees
    B. prefer charges against him
    C. transfer him to another school
    D. warn him that he must be on time

4. The one of the following procedures that is BEST to follow when it is necessary to reprimand a worker is to

    A. issue the same reprimand to all your men
    B. avoid him so he won't feel bad
    C. speak to him privately about the matter
    D. tell him what he has done wrong immediately to teach the other employees a lesson

5. The LEAST important factor to consider when evaluating the work of an employee is

    A. his grade on his civil service test
    B. the quality of his work
    C. his resourcefulness
    D. his attendance record

6. The one of the following supervisory actions that a custodian should use LEAST often is to   6.___

   A. make periodic reports to his superior about the work of his men
   B. bring employees up on "charges" whenever they do anything wrong
   C. listen to staff grievances
   D. advise an employee concerning a personal problem

7. The MAIN supervisory responsibility of a custodian is to   7.___

   A. foster policies of the board and the parents' organizations
   B. do his job so well that the students and employees like him
   C. make assignments to his employees
   D. keep the building and grounds in good operating condition

8. One of your employees verbally protests to you about your evaluation of his work. The BEST way to handle him is to   8.___

   A. advise him of your lengthy and qualified experience
   B. tell him that you do not care to talk about it
   C. explain to him how you arrived at your evaluation
   D. tell him that since all the other employees are satisfied, he should withdraw his complaint

9. A custodian will BEST keep the morale of his men high by   9.___

   A. giving praise for well-done work
   B. assigning good workers the most work
   C. personally helping each man in all the details of the man's job
   D. allowing special privileges for good work

10. In training maintenance personnel under the supervision of a custodian, the one of the following that should be given LEAST consideration by the custodian is   10.___

    A. how the training is to be given
    B. who is to be trained
    C. when the training will be given
    D. how the school principal wants them to be trained

11. The BEST attitude for a custodian to follow in his dealings with the public is to   11.___

    A. offer aid and cooperation to the public wherever possible
    B. show authority so that the public knows the limits to which they may make requests
    C. ignore the public since the custodian has a specific job to do
    D. refer the public to higher authority for solution of all their problems

12. The students playing in the schoolyard consistently lose rubber balls that land on the school roof. They request that you, the custodian, retrieve these balls
    Of the following, the BEST procedure for you to follow is .   12.___

    A. teach them a lesson and refuse to retrieve the balls
    B. retrieve the balls and throw them into the incinerator
    C. one day a week retrieve the balls and return them to the students
    D. retrieve the balls and give them to a local children's charity

13. The president of a charitable organization requests a permit to use the school building. You, the custodian, note that this same organization used the school previously and did not observe the "no smoking" rules.
    The BEST procedure for you to follow is to

    A. deny the organization a permit since they did not obey the school regulations before
    B. issue the permit without any questions since a large group is difficult to control
    C. inform the president that if any of his members continue to disregard the "no smoking" rules, future permits will not be issued
    D. inform the president that if any of his members continue to disregard the "no smoking" rules, you will evict them from the school building

14. Due to some grievances, parents occupy your school on a weekend and refuse to leave. As the school principal is out of town and unavailable, the BEST procedure for you, the custodian on duty, is to

    A. tell your employees to vacate the school
    B. call the police department
    C. cooperate with the parents on the take-over
    D. lock all the people in the school

15. An organization requests a permit to use the school auditorium from the hours of 7 P.M. to 10 P.M. on a Tuesday evening. The organization also requests that its members be allowed to enter the school earlier than 7 P.M. and leave later than 10 P.M.
    The BEST procedure for you, the custodian, to follow is to

    A. inform the organization leader that the organization may only use the school from the hours of 7 P.M. to 10 P.M.
    B. issue the permit without saying anything as you want to maintain good public relations
    C. refer the matter to the school principal as you do not want to get involved
    D. ask the organization leader the reasons for the request and, if the request is fair, issue the permit and let the organization do as it pleases

16. Dog owners in the neighborhood have been disregarding the *curb your dog* signs and walking their dogs on your school lawn. You find that this interferes with the operation of powered lawn mowing equipment.
    Your BEST procedure to follow is to

    A. put up a higher fence
    B. chase the people and dogs away
    C. tell the owners you will call the police department
    D. explain the problem to the owners and ask them to curb their dogs

17. A cleaner reports to the custodian that a particular schoolroom is consistently messy and dirty. The one who is equally at fault as the students for this dirty room is the

    A. students' parents
    B. regular classroom teacher
    C. student peer groups
    D. cleaner for reporting the matter

18. A parent walks into a custodian's office and starts to shout at him about a claimed injustice to her child. The PROPER procedure for the custodian to follow is to

    A. call the police department
    B. summon the security guards
    C. vacate the office
    D. escort the parent to a guidance counselor

19. A newspaper reporter visiting a school should normally be referred to the

    A. school principal
    B. school custodian engineer
    C. assistant superintendent of schools
    D. borough supervisor of school custodians

20. The parents of children in the neighborhood of your school complain to you that their children cannot use the school playground after school hours because the gates are closed.
    The BEST procedure for you to follow is

    A. tell the parents the gates will remain closed after school hours
    B. arrange for the children to use a play street
    C. tell the parents to meet with the board on this matter
    D. try to arrange for the school gates to be open to a later hour after school hours

21. Assume that there is a regulation requiring the men to notify the custodian when they intend to be absent. One of your men stays out without notifying you.
    Of the following, the FIRST thing that you should do is to

    A. discuss the matter with your supervisor
    B. find out the reason for the man's failure to comply with this regulation
    C. threaten the man with disciplinary action
    D. find out what the other custodians are doing about similar situations

22. The members of a crew are LEAST likely to object to strict rules as long as

    A. they know who made them
    B. the rules are applied only occasionally as a disciplinary measure
    C. the rules are applied equally to all the workers
    D. they are posted in a public place

23. Your supervisor complains to you that he could not find you at your assigned location and that the crew under your supervision was idle while you were away.
    Of the following, it is MOST important for you to

    A. improve your supervisory practices
    B. warn the men to look busy whenever they see one of the bosses
    C. disregard such an unreasonable complaint
    D. make certain you are rarely away from your assigned location

24. Assume that the crew you supervise considers some of their routine work unpleasant. The BEST way to get these unpleasant tasks done is to

    A. rotate them among all your men
    B. assign them to easygoing workers who never complain
    C. use them as a means of disciplining habitual latecomers
    D. do them yourself

25. Assume that when a custodian arrives at a job location, he finds that a loud argument is going on between two of his men.
    Of the following, the MOST advisable action for him to take first is to

    A. send one of the men to another job
    B. find out what caused the argument
    C. ask one of the other men to tell him the cause of the argument
    D. take the men with him to his supervisor

KEY (CORRECT ANSWERS)

1. A	11. A
2. B	12. C
3. D	13. C
4. C	14. B
5. A	15. A
6. B	16. D
7. D	17. B
8. C	18. D
9. A	19. A
10. D	20. D

21. B
22. C
23. A
24. A
25. B

TEST 2

DIRECTIONS: Each question or incomplete statement is followed by several suggested answers or completions. Select the one that BEST answers the question or completes the statement. *PRINT THE LETTER OF THE CORRECT ANSWER IN THE SPACE AT THE RIGHT.*

1. Of the following, the BEST reason for a custodian NOT allowing his employees to accept tips from people is that

    A. all employees would not be given equal treatment
    B. employees would become dishonest
    C. people are entitled to service without tips
    D. people in projects can't afford tips

    1.___

2. Your attitude as a custodian to complaints by your employees should be that

    A. all employees like to complain
    B. if you let the worker "give off some steam," the complaint will disappear
    C. you will listen to them and try to correct the condition
    D. you will try to show the worker where he is wrong

    2.___

3. A requisition would be filled out by a custodian in order to

    A. get supplies from the stockroom
    B. return to the stockroom supplies you haven't used
    C. find out the supplies you have on hand
    D. show that supplies were used up faster than expected

    3.___

4. Assume that you are a custodian and have to write a report on a new employee who will finish his probationary period next month.
Which one of the following would be the BEST reason for recommending that he be dropped from the job? He

    A. was late several times during the past five months for a total of 50 minutes
    B. is a slow worker compared to the other men
    C. insists on eating his lunch alone instead of with the other men
    D. is in the habit of accepting drinks from outsiders during working hours although you have often told him it is forbidden

    4.___

5. It is MOST important that a report from a custodian to his superior be

    A. typewritten
    B. free of any mistakes in spelling or English
    C. accurate and have all the necessary facts
    D. brief to save time of all concerned

    5.___

6. Suppose that you are a custodian and one of your men asks why you did not recommend him for an above-average work performance rating.
You should tell him

    A. that above-average work reports can be recommended only by higher authority
    B. why you did not give him an above-average work report
    C. that you will recommend an above-average v/ork performance rating next year if he does better work
    D. how he can appeal his rating and help him write his appeal

    6.___

7. Suppose that you are a custodian and one of your men is absent from work one day. You don't have any extra men and some of the work usually done by the absent man has to be finished that day.
   It would be BEST for you to

   A. call your men together and let them decide which one is to do the work
   B. shorten the lunch period and have each man do some of the work
   C. ask one of your better men to *pitch in* by doing a little extra work today
   D. explain to the buildings superintendent why it will not be possible to finish this work today

8. One of your men complains about a job you gave him. He is angry about getting the assignment. You don't think that the man is right in getting so upset.
   You should

   A. discuss the problem with him and explain why you gave him the job
   B. refer the man to your supervisor because he refuses to obey orders
   C. show the man that the whole matter is unimportant and a waste of time
   D. tell the man to do the job first and complain later

9. Two of your men start an argument while at work. As a custodian, you should

   A. ignore them; it is normal for men working together to have arguments
   B. stop them right away and find out what started the argument
   C. let them argue it out as long as they continue working and don't talk too loud
   D. speak to one of the men privately and tell him he is interfering with the work

10. Suppose you are a new custodian and you are put in charge of a crew of men whom you do not know and who have been working together for a few months.
    For a smooth changeover to your leadership, it would be BEST for you to

    A. let them continue working at their present assignments while you get to know them better
    B. tell the men to call their old supervisor if they have any trouble while you are learning the job
    C. ask the most experienced man to take charge of the crew for a short while until you are more familiar with the work
    D. ask each man whether he is satisfied with what he is doing or wants a change

11. One of your men makes a suggestion for improving the method of doing the work. You don't think the suggestion is workable.
    You should, as a custodian,

    A. forget the idea since it isn't workable
    B. tell the man to try out the idea and hold him responsible if it doesn't work out
    C. discuss with the man why you think the idea won't work and praise him for his interest in the job
    D. point out to the man that he is wasting your time bringing up an idea that is not practical

12. Suppose that you and your supervisor are making an inspection of one of the buildings you are responsible for cleaning. Your superior notices that the elevator in the building has not been cleaned. You know that a new employee who has been on the job for only three months is assigned
to this building. You should

    A. tell your supervisor that you will have the elevator cleaned and see that it is kept clean in the future
    B. explain to your supervisor the trouble you have in training new employees
    C. find the new man and ask him to explain to you and your superior why the elevator is not clean
    D. tell your supervisor that the elevator was clean when you made your last inspection

13. Suppose that your men were asked to work overtime in order to repair a water main break. When the work is finished, your superior thanks you for the excellent work that was done.
For you, a custodian, to tell your men about this would be

    A. *bad,* because this was a private conversation between you and your superior
    B. *good,* because your men will see that you are well-liked by your superior
    C. *bad,* because your men will think that they will be asked to work whenever there is an emergency
    D. *good,* because it will show the men their cooperation is appreciated

14. When you, as a custodian, discuss a grievance with an employee, you should

    A. not tell the employee what you think of his complaint until a later date
    B. avoid any arguments with the employee
    C. convince the employee that there is no basis for this grievance
    D. tell the employee his complaint is justified

15. At a quarter to five, one of your employees tells you that the incinerator in his building has much refuse in it and he is willing to work overtime to burn it.
If you give him permission to do this, it would be

    A. *good,* because it will save time the next day for other important work
    B. *bad,* because this is not an emergency for which overtime could be approved
    C. *good,* because tenants would not complain that refuse piles up and causes odors
    D. *bad,* because the law does not allow burning after 5:00 P.M.

16. Because of absences, you are left short-handed.
Which one of the following operations should you lay over so that you can cover the MOST important work on a minimum basis?

    A. Incineration of garbage
    B. Sweeping the lobby
    C. Sweeping and washing the elevators
    D. Washing corridor windows

17. Suppose that one of your men who is doing good work asks for a transfer to another custodian.
    It would be BEST for you to

    A. have a private talk with the man to find out why he wants a transfer
    B. tell the man that the other custodian will also expect him to do good work
    C. approve the transfer without question because a dissatisfied man will do a poor job
    D. ask the other men in your crew if they are dissatisfied with your supervision

    17.____

18. One of your experienced workers and a new employee are arguing about the correct way to do a job on which they are working together.
    As a custodian, you should

    A. listen to both men and then tell them that they must learn to settle their argument without interrupting your work
    B. side with the older worker because he is more experienced
    C. listen to both men and then tell them how the work is to be done
    D. take one of the men off the job

    18.____

19. Suppose that the department is introducing a new procedure for cleaning the hallways of buildings.
    As a custodian, the BEST way for you to acquaint your men with this new procedure and to get them to use it is to

    A. wait until it has been tried out in another building and, if it is successful, put it into use in your building
    B. give each man a printed copy of the new procedure and set a deadline date by which each man is to read it and know it
    C. get your men together and explain the new procedure to them and how it will affect their work
    D. teach it to your best man and when he is familiar with it, ask him to teach it to the other men one at a time

    19.____

20. Suppose that, as a custodian, you have finished *breaking in* a new employee. A few days later, you see the new man doing the job the wrong way.
    You should

    A. immediately show the man what he is doing wrong and how to do it correctly
    B. assign him to some other work
    C. let your superior know that the new man cannot follow instructions
    D. say nothing because you may make the new man nervous

    20.____

21. Suppose that a new type waxing machine is to be used in your building.
    Of the following, the BEST way for you to teach your men how to use this machine is to

    A. give a talk on how to operate the machine
    B. demonstrate the operation and then have each man operate the machine under your supervision
    C. have the manufacturer give a talk on how to operate the machine
    D. give each man a set of carefully written instructions on how to operate the machine

    21.____

22. When a custodian has to teach a man a new job, it would be MOST helpful for him to find out

    A. how long the man has been with the department and how long he plans to stay
    B. the man's dependability and willingness
    C. the man's past record of cooperation with other workers
    D. what the man already knows that will help him in learning the new job

23. When a new custodian comes on the job, it is LEAST important for him to know

    A. the location of the buildings in the unit
    B. how long the foremen have been there
    C. the names of the men who work there
    D. where the tools and equipment are kept

24. When you assign work to your men, it is usually BEST to

    A. give each man the same amount of work
    B. give the jobs that take the longest time to the senior men
    C. assign work to each man according to his ability
    D. let each man pick his own assignment

25. As a custodian, you will MOST likely be respected by your men if you

    A. keep your personnel records simple and clear
    B. offer them advice in solving their family problems
    C. leave it to them to decide how a job is to be done
    D. are fair and honest with them

KEY (CORRECT ANSWERS)

1.	C	11.	C
2.	C	12.	A
3.	A	13.	D
4.	D	14.	B
5.	C	15.	D
6.	B	16.	D
7.	C	17.	A
8.	A	18.	C
9.	B	19.	C
10.	A	20.	A

21. B
22. D
23. B
24. C
25. D

TEST 3

DIRECTIONS: Each question or incomplete statement is followed by several suggested answers or completions. Select the one that BEST answers the question or completes the statement. *PRINT THE LETTER OF THE CORRECT ANSWER IN THE SPACE AT THE RIGHT.*

1. Good public relations can be damaged by a custodian who treats tenants, fellow workers, friends, relatives, and the public with

   A. courtesy
   B. consideration
   C. contempt
   D. respect

   1.___

2. An office worker complains to a custodian that one of the cleaners broke off a branch of a plant which she kept on her desk and that she can identify the cleaner.
   The BEST thing for the custodian to do is to

   A. convince her that the plant will grow another branch eventually
   B. make the cleaner apologize and pay for a new plant out of his own pocket
   C. sympathize with the office worker and assure her that he will speak to the cleaner about it
   D. tell her not to bother him about her personal property

   2.___

3. When a new employee reports to a custodian on his first day on the job, the custodian SHOULD

   A. extend a hearty welcome and make the new employee feel welcome
   B. have the man sit and wait for a while before seeing him so that the employee realizes how busy the custodian is
   C. warn him of stern disciplinary action if he is late or absent excessively
   D. tell him he probably will have difficulty doing the work so that he doesn't become overconfident

   3.___

4. The one of the following subjects of a fire prevention training program which is MOST readily applied on the job is the

   A. elimination of fire hazards
   B. use of portable fire extinguishers
   C. knowledge of types of fires
   D. method of reporting fires

   4.___

5. A custodian who is a good supervisor will NOT

   A. tell his men what their jobs are and why they are important
   B. show his men how their jobs are to be done in the right way
   C. require some of the men to do their jobs in the presence of the supervisor demonstrating that they understand the job
   D. leave his men alone because they will always do their jobs correctly once they have received their instructions

   5.___

6. When a custodian sees a worker doing his job incorrectly, he should

   A. tell the worker to be more careful
   B. suspend the worker until he learns to do the job correctly
   C. tell the worker specifically how the job should be done
   D. scold the man

   6.___

7. An employee who is a good worker but is often late for work

   A. is lazy and should be dismissed
   B. cannot tell time
   C. can have no excuse for being late more than once a month
   D. should be questioned by his supervisor to try to find out why he is late

8. When starting any disciplinary action, a custodian who is a good supervisor should

   A. show his annoyance by losing his temper
   B. be apologetic
   C. be sarcastic
   D. be firm and positive

9. The BEST way for a custodian to maintain good employee morale is to

   A. avoid praising any one employee
   B. always have an alibi for his own mistakes
   C. encourage cliques by giving them information before giving it to other workers
   D. give adequate credit and praise when due

10. The BEST way for a custodian to tell if the night cleaners have done their work well is to check

    A. on how much cleaning material has been used
    B. on how much waste paper was collected
    C. the building for cleanliness
    D. the floor mops to see if they are still wet

11. The one of the following which is the BEST reason for introducing a training program is that the

    A. quality of work is above standard
    B. employees are all experienced
    C. accident rate is too high
    D. complaints are negligible

12. The FIRST step in training an inexperienced individual in a particular job is to

    A. put him to work and watch for mistakes
    B. put him to work and tell him to call for help if he needs it
    C. put him at ease and then find out what he knows about the work
    D. tell him to watch the least experienced worker on the job because the training is still fresh in his mind

13. As used in job analysis, the term *job breakdown* means

    A. any equipment failure
    B. any failure on the part of the worker to complete the job
    C. dividing the job into a series of steps
    D. reducing the number of workers by 50 percent

14. In dealing with the public, a custodian should be

    A. indulgent
    B. courteous
    C. disagreeable
    D. unavailable

15. If a custodian sees a group of people in front of his building preparing to form a picket line, he should

    A. turn on a lawn sprinkler to spray the pickets
    B. order the pickets off the sidewalk in front of the building
    C. show the pickets he is sympathetic with their complaint against the city
    D. contact his supervisor immediately for instructions

16. When electric service in a public building is to be shut off from 10 A.M. Tuesday to 11:30 the next morning because a new electric feeder cable is being installed, the custodian should

    A. prepare a memo to all office supervisors in the building, notifying them of the situation, and deliver a copy to each office as soon as possible
    B. prepare a notice of the impending power stoppage and post it in the lobby early Tuesday morning
    C. tell the electrical contractor to notify the tenants when he is about to shut off the power
    D. discontinue elevator service at 10 A.M. on Tuesday as an indication to the tenants that the power supply is off

17. Time standards for cleaning are of value ONLY if

    A. a bonus is promised if the time standards are beaten
    B. the cleaners determine the methods and procedures to be used
    C. accompanied by a completely detailed description of the methods to be used
    D. a schematic diagram of the area is made available to the cleaners

18. Of the following, the one which is the LEAST important factor in deciding that additional training is necessary for the men you supervise is that

    A. the quality of work is below standard
    B. supplies are being wasted
    C. too much time is required to do specific jobs
    D. the absentee rate has declined

19. To promote proper safety practices in the operation of power tools and equipment, the custodian should emphasize in meetings with his staff that

    A. every accident can be prevented through proper safety regulations
    B. proper safety practices will probably make future safety meetings unnecessary
    C. when safety rules are followed, tools and equipment will work better
    D. safety rules are based on past experience with the best methods of preventing accidents

20. As a custodian, a GOOD practical method to use in determining whether an employee is doing his job properly is to

    A. assume that if he asks no questions, he knows the work
    B. question him directly on details of the job
    C. inspect and follow-up the work which is assigned to him
    D. ask other employees how this employee is making out

21. If an employee continually asks how he should do his work, the custodian should

    A. dismiss him immediately
    B. pretend he does not hear him unless he persists
    C. explain the work carefully but encourage him to use his own judgment
    D. tell him not to ask so many questions

22. As a custodian, you have instructed an employee to wet mop a certain area. To be sure that the employee understands the instructions you have given him, you should

    A. ask him to repeat the instructions to you
    B. check with him after he has done the job
    C. watch him while he is doing the job
    D. repeat the instructions to the employee

23. As a custodian, one of your men disagrees with your evaluation of his work. Of the following, the BEST way to handle this situation would be to

    A. explain that you are in a better position to evaluate his work than he is
    B. tell him that since the other men are satisfied with your evaluation, he should accept their opinions
    C. explain the basis of your evaluation and discuss it with him
    D. refuse to discuss his complaint in order to maintain discipline

24. Of the following, the one which is NOT a purpose of a cleaning job breakdown is to

    A. eliminate unnecessary steps
    B. determine the type of floor wax to use
    C. rearrange the sequence of operations to save time
    D. combine steps or actions where practicable

25. The BEST method of making cleaning assignments in a large building is by means of

    A. daily rotation
    B. specific assignment
    C. individual choice
    D. chronological order

KEY (CORRECT ANSWERS)

1. C
2. C
3. A
4. A
5. D

6. C
7. D
8. D
9. D
10. C

11. C
12. C
13. C
14. B
15. D

16. A
17. C
18. D
19. D
20. C

21. C
22. A
23. C
24. B
25. B

EXAMINATION SECTION
TEST 1

DIRECTIONS: Each question or incomplete statement is followed by several suggested answers or completions. Select the one that BEST answers the question or completes the statement. *PRINT THE LETTER OF THE CORRECT ANSWER IN THE SPACE AT THE RIGHT.*

1. A supervisor was given a booklet that showed a new work method that could save time. He didn't tell his men because he thought that they would get the booklet anyway.
   For the supervisor to have acted like this is a
   A. *good* idea, because he saves time and both of talking to the men
   B. *bad* idea, because he should make sure his men know about better work methods
   C. *good* idea, because the men would rather read about it themselves
   D *bad* idea, because a supervisor should always show his men every memo he gets from higher authority

1.____

2. A supervisor found it necessary to discipline two subordinates. One man had been operating his equipment in a wrong way, while the other man came to work late for three days in a row. The supervisor decided to talk to both men together.
   For the supervisor to deal with the problems in this way is a
   A. *good* idea because each man will learn about the difficulties of the other person and how to solve such difficulties
   B. *bad* idea because the supervisor should wait until he can bring a larger group together and save time in discussing such questions
   C. *good* idea because he will be able to get the men to see that their problems are related
   D. *bad* idea because he should meet with each man separately and give him his full attention

2.____

3. A supervisor should try to make his men feel their jobs are important in order to
   A. get the men to say good things about their supervisor to his own superior
   B. get the men to think in terms of advancing to better jobs
   C. let higher management in the agency know that the supervisor is efficient
   D. help the men to be able to work more efficiently and enthusiastically

3.____

4. A supervisor should know approximately how long it takes to do a particular kind of job CHIEFLY because he
   A. will know how much time to take if he has to do it himself
   B. will be able to tell his men to do it even faster
   C. can judge the performance of the person doing the job
   D. can retrain experienced employees in better work habits

4.____

109

5. Supervisors often get their employees' opinions about better work methods because
   A. the men will know that they are respected
   B. the men would otherwise lose all their confidence in the supervisor
   C. the supervisor might find in this way a good suggestion he could use
   D. this is the best method for improvement of work methods

6. Right after you have trained your subordinates in doing a new job, you find that they seem to be doing all right, but that it will take them several days to finish. You also have several groups of men working at other locations.
   The MOST efficient way for you to make sure that the men continue doing the new job properly is to
   A. stay on that job with the men until it is finished just in case trouble develops
   B. visit the men every half hour until the job is done
   C. stay away from their job that day and visit the men the next day to ask them if they had any problems
   D. visit the men a few times each day until they finish the new job

7. Assume that one of your new employees is older than you are. You also think that he may be hard to get along with because he is older than you.
   The BEST way for you to avoid any problems with the older worker is for you to
   A. lay down the law immediately and tell the man he better not cause you any trouble
   B. treat the man just the way you would any other worker
   C. always ask the older worker for advice in the presence of all the men
   D. ignore the man entirely until he realizes that you are the boss

8. Assume that you have tried a new method suggested by one of your employees and find that it is easier and cheaper than the method you had been using.
   The PROPER thing for you to do NEXT is to
   A. say nothing to anyone but train your men to use the new method
   B. train your men to use the new method and tell your crew that you got the idea from one of the men
   C. continue using the old method because a supervisor should not use suggestions of his men
   D. have your crew learn the new method and take credit for the idea since you are the boss

9. Suppose you are a supervisor and your superior tells you that the way your men are doing a certain procedure is wrong and that you should re-train our men as soon as possible.
   When you begin to re-train the men, the FIRST thing you should do is to
   A. tell your men that a wrong procedure had been used and that a new method must be learned as a result
   B. train your employees in the new method with no explanation since you are the boss

C. tell the crew that your superior has just decided that everyone should learn a new method
D. tell the crew that your superior says your method is wrong but that you don't agree with this

10. It is BAD practice to criticize a man in front of the other men because
    A. people will think you are too strict
    B. it is annoying to anyone who walks by
    C. it is embarrassing to the man concerned
    D. it will antagonize the other men

10._____

11. A supervisor decides not to put his two best men on a work detail because he knows that they won't like it.
    For the supervisor to make the work assignment this way is a
    A. *good* idea because it is only fair to give your best men a break once in a while
    B. *bad* idea because you should treat all of your me fairly and not show favoritism
    C. *good* idea because you save the strength of these men for another job
    D. *bad* idea because more of the men should be exempted from the assignment

11._____

12. Suppose you are a supervisor and you find it inconvenient to obey an established procedure set by your agency. You think another procedure would be better.
    The BEST thing to do first about this procedure that you don't like is for you to
    A. obey the procedure even if you don't to and suggest your idea to your own supervisor
    B. disregard the procedure because a supervisor is supposed to have some privileges
    C. follow the procedure some of the time but ignore it when the men are not watching
    D. organize a group of other supervisors to get the procedure changed

12._____

13. A supervisor estimated that it would take his crew one workday per week to do a certain job each week. However, after a month he noticed that the job averaged two and a half days a week and this delayed other jobs that had to be done.
    The FIRST thing that the supervisor should do in this case is to
    A. call him men together and warn them that they will get a poor work evaluation if they do not work harder
    B. talk to each man personally, asking him to work harder on the job
    C. go back and study the maintenance job by himself to see if more men should be assigned to the job
    D. write his boss a report describing in detail how much time it is taking the men to do the job

13._____

14. An employee complains to you that some of the work assignments are too difficult to do alone.
    Which of the following is the BEST way for you to handle this complaint?
    A. Go with him to see exactly what he does and why he finds it so difficult
    B. Politely tell the man that he has to do the job or be brought up on charges
    C. Tell the man to send his complaint to the head of your agency
    D. Sympathize with the man and give him easier jobs

15. The BEST way for a supervisor to keep control of his work assignments is to
    A. ask the men to report to him immediately when their jobs are finished
    B. walk around the buildings once a week and get a first-hand view of what is being done
    C. keep his ears open for problems and complaints, but leave the men aloe to do the work
    D. write up a work schedule and check it periodically against the actual work done

16. A supervisor made a work schedule for his men. At the bottom of it, he wrote, *No changes or exceptions will be made in this schedule for any reason.*
    For the supervisor to have made this statement is
    A. *good*, because the men will respect the supervisor for his attitude
    B. *bad*, because there are emergencies and special situations that occur
    C. *good*, because each man will know exactly what is expected of him
    D. *bad*, because the men should expect that no changes will ever be made in the work schedule without written permission

17. Which one of the following would NOT be a result of a well-planned work schedule?
    The schedule
    A. makes efficient use of the time of the staff
    B. acts as a checklist for an important job that might be left out
    C. will give an idea of the work to a substitute supervisor
    D. shows at a glance who the best men are

18. A new piece of equipment you have ordered is delivered. You are familiar with it, but the men under you who will use it do not know the equipment.
    Of the following methods, which is the BEST to take in explaining to them how to operate this equipment?
    A. Ask the men to watch other crews using the equipment
    B. Show one reliable man how to operate the equipment and ask him to teach the other men
    C. Ask the men to read the instructions in the manual for the equipment
    D. Call the men together and show them how to operate the equipment

19. One supervisor assigns work to his men by calling his crew together each week and describing what has to be done that week. He then tells them to arrange individual assignments among themselves and to work as a team during the week.

This method of scheduling work is a
- A. *good* idea because this guarantees that the men will work together
- B. *bad* idea because responsibility for doing the job is poorly fixed
- C. *good* idea because the men will finish the job in less time, working together
- D. *bad* idea because the supervisor should always stay with his men

20. Suppose that an employee came to his supervisor with a problem concerning his assignment.
    For the supervisor to listen to his problem is a
    - A. *good* idea because a supervisor should always take time off to talk when one of his men wants to talk
    - B. *bad* idea because the supervisor should not be bothered during the work day
    - C. *good* idea because it is the job of the supervisor to deal with problems of job assignment
    - D. *bad* idea because the employee could start annoying the supervisor with all sorts of problems

20.____

21. Suppose that on the previous afternoon you were looking for an experienced employee in order to give him an emergency job and he was missing from his job location. The next morning, he tells you that he got sick suddenly and had to go home, but could not tell you since you were not around. He has never done this before.
    What should you do?
    - A. Tell the man he is excused and that in such circumstances he did the wisest thing
    - B. Bring the man up on charges because whatever he says he could still have notified you
    - C. Have the man examined by a doctor to see if he really was sick the day before
    - D. Explain to the mean that he should make every effort to tell you or to get a message to you if he must leave

21.____

22. An employee had a grievance and went to his supervisor about it. The employee was not satisfied with the way the supervisor tried to help him and told him so. Yet, the supervisor had done everything he could under the circumstances.
    The PROPER action for the supervisor to take at this time is to
    - A. politely tell the employee that there is nothing more for the supervisor to do about the problem
    - B. let the employee know how he can bring his complaint to a higher authority
    - C. tell the employee that he must solve the problem on his own since he did not want to follow the supervisor's advice
    - D. suggest to the employee that he ask for another supervisor for assistance

22.____

23. In which of the following situations is it BEST to give your men spoken rather than written orders?
    A. You want your men to have a record of the instructions.
    B. Spoken instructions are less likely to be forgotten.
    C. An emergency situation has arisen in which there is no time to write up instructions.
    D. There are instructions on time and leave regulations which are complicated.

24. One of your employees tells you that a week ago he had a small accident on the job but he did not bother telling you because he was able to continue working.
    For the employee not to have told his supervisor about the accident was
    A. *good*, because the accident was a small one
    B. *bad*, because all accidents should be reported, no matter how small
    C. *good*, because the supervisor should be bothered only for important matters
    D. *bad*, because having an accident is one way to get excused for the day

25. For a supervisor to deal with each of his subordinate in exactly the same manner is
    A. *poor*, because each man presents a different problem and there is no one way of handling all problems
    B. *good*, because once a problem is handled with one man, he can handle another man with the same problem
    C. *poor*, because the men will resent it if they are not handled each in a better way than others
    D. *good*, because this assures fair and impartial treatment of each subordinate

KEY (CORRECT ANSWERS)

1.	B	11.	B
2.	D	12.	A
3.	D	13.	C
4.	C	14.	A
5.	C	15.	D
6.	D	16.	B
7.	B	17.	D
8.	B	18.	D
9.	A	19.	B
10.	C	20.	C

21. D
22. B
23. C
24. B
25. A

TEST 2

DIRECTIONS: Each question or incomplete statement is followed by several suggested answers or completions. Select the one that BEST answers the question or completes the statement. *PRINT THE LETTER OF THE CORRECT ANSWER IN THE SPACE AT THE RIGHT.*

1. Jim Johnson has been on your staff for over four years. He has always been a conscientious and productive worker. About a month ago, his wife died; and since that time, his work performance has been very poor.
   As his supervisor, which one of the following is the BEST way for you to deal with this situation?
   A. Allow Jim as much time as he needs to overcome his grief and hope that his work performance improves
   B. Meet with Jim to discuss ways to improve his performance
   C. Tell Jim directly that you are more concerned with his work performance than with his personal problem
   D. Prepare disciplinary action on Jim as soon as possible

   1._____

2. You are responsible for the overall operation of a storehouse which is divided into two sections. Each section has its own supervisor. You have decided to make several complex changes in the storekeeping procedures which will affect both sections.
   Of the following, the BEST way to make sure that these changes are understood by the two supervisors is for you to
   A. meet with both supervisors to discuss the changes
   B. issue a memorandum to each supervisor explaining the changes
   C. post the changes where the supervisors are sure to see them
   D. instruct one supervisor to explain the changes to the other supervisor

   2._____

3. You have called a meeting of all your subordinates to tell them what has to be done on a new project in which they will all be involved. Several times during the meeting, you ask if there are any questions about what you have told them.
   Of the following, to ask the subordinates whether there are any questions during the meeting can BEST be described as
   A. *inadvisable*, because it interferes with their learning about the new project
   B. *advisable*, because you will find out what they don't understand and have a chance to clear up any problems they may have
   C. *inadvisable*, because it makes the meeting too long and causes the subordinates to lose interest in the new project
   D. *advisable*, because it gives you a chance to learn which of your subordinates are paying attention to what you say

   3._____

4. As a supervisor, you are responsible for seeing to it that absenteeism does not become a problem among your subordinates.
   Which one of the following is NOT an acceptable way of controlling the problem of excessive absences?

   4._____

A. Distribute a written statement to your staff on the policies regarding absenteeism in your organization
B. Arrange for workers who have the fewest absences to talk to those workers who have the most absences
C. Let your subordinates know that a record is being kept of all absences
D. Arrange for counseling of those employees who are frequently absent

5. One of your supervisors has been an excellent worker for the past two years. There are no promotion opportunities for this worker in the foreseeable future. Due to the city's present budget crisis, a salary increase is not possible.
Under the circumstances, which one of the following actions on your part would be MOST likely to continue to motivate this worker?
    A. Tell the worker that times are bad all over and jobs are hard to find
    B. Give the worker less work and easier assignments
    C. Tell the worker to try to look for a better paying job elsewhere
    D. Seek the worker's advice often and show that the suggestions provided are appreciated

6. As a supervisor in a warehouse, it is important that you use your available work force to its fullest potential.
Which one of the following actions on your part is MOST likely to increase the effectiveness of your work force?
    A. Assigning more workers to a job than the number actually needed
    B. Eliminating all job training to allow more time for work output
    C. Using your best workers on jobs that average workers can do
    D. Making sure that all materials and equipment used are maintained in good working order

7. You learn that your storage area will soon be undergoing changes which will affect the work of your subordinates. You decide not to tell your subordinates about what is to happen.
Of the following, your action can BEST be described as
    A. *wise*, because your subordinates will learn of the changes for themselves
    B. *unwise*, because your subordinates should be advised about what is to happen
    C. *wise*, because it is better for your subordinates to continue working without being disturbed by such news
    D. *unwise*, because the work of your subordinates will gradually slow down

8. In making plans for the operation of your unit, you are MOST likely to see these plans carried out successfully if you
    A. allow your staff to participate in developing these plans
    B. do not spend any time on the minor details of these plans
    C. base these plans on the past experiences of others
    D. allow these plans to interact with outside activities in other units

3 (#2)

9. As a supervisor in charge of the total operation of a food supply warehouse, you find vandalism to be a potentially serious problem. On occasion, trespassers have gained entrance into the facility by climbing over an unprotected 8-foot fence surrounding the warehouse whose dimensions measure 100 feet by 100 feet.
Assuming that all of the following would be equally effective ways in preventing these breaches in security in the situation described above, which one would be LEAST costly?
    A. Using two trained guard dogs to roam freely throughout the facility at night
    B. Hiring a security guard to patrol the facility after working hours
    C. Installing tape razor wire on top of the fence surrounding the facility
    D. Installing an electronic burglar alarm system requiring the installation of a new fence

9._____

10. The area for which you have program responsibility has undergone recent changes. Your staff is now required to perform many new tasks, and morale is low.
The LEAST effective way for you to improve long-term staff morale would be to
    A. develop support groups to discuss problems
    B. involve staff in job development
    C. maintain a comfortable social environment within the group
    D. adequately plan and give assignments in a timely manner

10._____

11. As a supervisor in a large office, one of your subordinate supervisors stops you in the middle of the office and complains loudly that he is being treated unfairly. The rest of the staff ceases work and listens to the complaint.
The MOST appropriate action for you to take in this situation is to
    A. ignore this unprofessional behavior and continue on your way
    B. tell the supervisor that his behavior is unprofessional and he should learn how to conduct himself
    C. explain to the supervisor why you believe he is not being treated unfairly
    D. ask the supervisor to come to your office at a specific time to discuss the matter

11._____

12. You are told that one of your subordinates is distributing literature which attempts to recruit individuals to join a particular organization. Several workers complain that their rights are being violated.
Of the following, the BEST action for you to take FIRST is to
    A. ignore the situation because no harm is being done
    B. discuss the matter further with your supervisor
    C. ask the worker to stop distributing the literature
    D. tell the workers that they do not have to read the material

12._____

13. You have been assigned to develop a short training course for a recently issued procedure.
In designing this course, which of the following statements is the LEAST important for you to consider?

13._____

A. The learning experience must be interesting and meaningful in terms of the staff member's job.
B. The method of teaching must be strictly followed in order to develop successful learning experiences.
C. The course content should incorporate the rules and regulations of the agency.
D. The procedure should be consistent with the agency's objectives.

14. As a supervisor, there are several newly-promoted employees under your supervision. Each of these employees is subject to a probationary period PRIMARILY to
    A. assess the employee's performance to see if the employee should be retained or removed from the position
    B. give the employee the option to return to his former employment if the employee is unhappy in the new position
    C. give the employee an opportunity to learn the duties and responsibilities of the position
    D. judge the employee's potential for upward mobility in the future

15. An employee under your supervision rushes into your office to tell you he has just received a telephone bomb threat.
    As the administrative supervisor, the FIRST thing you should do is
    A. evacuate staff from the floor
    B. call the police and building security
    C. advise your administrator
    D. do a preliminary search

16. After reviewing the Absence Control form for a unit under your supervision, you find that one of your staff members has a fifth undocumented sick leave within a six-month period.
    In this situation, the FIRST action you should take is to
    A. discuss the seriousness of the matter with the staff member when he returns to work and fully document the details of the discussion
    B. review the case with the location director and warn the staff member that future use of sick leave will be punished
    C. submit the proper disciplinary forms to ensure that the staff member is penalized for excessive absences
    D. request that the timekeeper put the staff member on doctor's note restriction

17. A subordinate supervisor recently assigned to your office begins his first conference with you by saying that he has learned something that another supervisor is doing that you should know about.
    After hearing this statement, of the following, the BEST approach for you to take is to
    A. explain to the supervisor that the conference is to discuss his work and not that of his co-workers
    B. tell the supervisor that you do not encourage a spy system among the staff you supervise

C. tell the supervisor that you will listen to his report only if the other supervisor is present
D. allow the supervisor to continue talking until you have enough information to make a decision on how best to respond

18. Assume that you are a supervisor recently assigned to a new unit. You notice that, for the past few days, one of the employees in your unit whose work is about average has been stopping work at about four o'clock and has been spending the rest of the afternoon relaxing at his desk.
The BEST of the following actions for you to take in this situation is to
   A. assign more work to this employee since it is apparent that he does not have enough work to keep him busy
   B. observe the employee's conduct more closely for about ten days before taking any more positive action
   C. discuss the matter with the employee, pointing out to him how he can use the extra hour daily to raise the level of his job performance
   D. question the previous supervisor in charge of the unit in order to determine whether he had sanctioned such conduct when he supervised that unit

19. A new supervisor was assigned to your program four months ago. Although he tries hard, he has been unable to meet certain standards because he still has a lot to learn. As his supervisor, you are required to submit performance evaluations within a few days.
How would you rate this employee on the tasks where he fails to meet standards because of lack of experience?
   A. Satisfactory
   B. Conditional
   C. Unsatisfactory
   D. Unratable

20. You find that there is an important procedural error in a memo which you distributed to your staff several days ago.
The BEST approach for you to take at this time is to
   A. send a corrected memo to the staff, indicating what prior error was made
   B. send a corrected memo to the staff without mentioning the prior error
   C. tell the staff about the error at the next monthly staff meeting
   D. place the corrected memo on the office bulletin board

21. Your superior asks you, a supervisor, about the status of the response to a letter from a public official concerning a client's case. When you ask the subordinate who was assigned to prepare the response to give you the letter, the subordinate denies that it was given to him. You are certain that the subordinate has the letter, but is withholding it because the response has not yet been prepared.
Of the following, in order to secure the letter from the subordinate, you should FIRST
   A. accuse the subordinate of lying and demand that the letter be given to you immediately
   B. say that you would consider it a personal favor if the subordinate would find the letter

6 (#2)

    C. continue to question the subordinate until he admits to having been given the letter
    D. offer a face-saving solution, such as asking the subordinate to look again for the letter

22. As a supervisor, you have been assigned to write a few paragraphs to be included in the agency's annual report, describing a public service agency department this year as compared to last year.
Which of the following elements basic to the agency is LEAST likely to have changed since last year?
    A. Mission   B. Structure   C. Technology   D. Personnel

22.____

23. As a supervisor, you have been informed that a grievance has been filed against you, accusing you of assigning a subordinate to out-of-title tasks.
Of the following, the BEST approach for you to take is to
    A. waive the grievance so that it will proceed to a Step II hearing
    B. immediately change the subordinate's assignment to avoid future problems
    C. respond to the grievance, giving appropriate reasons for the assignment
    D. review the job description to ensure that the subordinate's tasks are not out-of-title

23.____

24. Which of the following is NOT a correct statement about agency group training programs in a public service agency?
    A. Training sessions continue for an indefinite period of time.
    B. Group training sessions are planned for designated personnel.
    C. Training groups are organized formally through administrative planning.
    D. Group training is task-centered and aimed toward accomplishing specific educational goals.

24.____

25. As a supervisor, you have submitted a memo to your superior requesting a conference to discuss the performance of a manager under your supervision. The memo states that the manager has a good working relationship with her staff; however, she tends to interpret agency policy too liberally and shows poor administrative skills by missing some deadlines and not keeping proper controls.
Which of the following steps should NOT be taken in order to prepare for this conference with your superior?
    A. Collect and review all your notes regarding the manager's prior performance.
    B. Outline your agenda so that you will have sufficient time to discuss the situation.
    C. Tell the manager that you will be discussing her performance with your superior.
    D. Clearly define objectives which will focus on improving the manager's performance.

25.____

7 (#2)

KEY (CORRECT ANSWERS)

1.	B		11.	D
2.	A		12.	C
3.	B		13.	B
4.	B		14.	A
5.	D		15.	B
6.	D		16.	A
7.	B		17.	D
8.	A		18.	C
9.	C		19.	B
10.	C		20.	A

21. D
22. A
23. C
24. A
25. C

READING COMPREHENSION
UNDERSTANDING AND INTERPRETING WRITTEN MATERIAL
EXAMINATION SECTION
TEST 1

DIRECTIONS: Each question or incomplete statement is followed by several suggested answers or completions. Select the one that BEST answers the question or completes the statement. *PRINT THE LETTER OF THE CORRECT ANSWER IN THE SPACE AT THE RIGHT.*

Questions 1-3.

DIRECTIONS: Questions 1 through 3 are to be answered in accordance with the following passage.

    Terrazzo flooring will last a very long time if it is cared for properly. Lacquers, shellac, or varnish preparations should never be used on terrazzo. Soap cleaners are not recommended since they dull the appearance of the floor. Alkaline solutions are harmful, so a neutral cleaner or non-alkaline synthetic detergents will give best results. If the floor is very dirty, it may be necessary to scrub it. The same neutral cleaning solution should be used for scrubbing as for mopping. Scouring powder may be sprinkled at particularly dirty spots. Do not use steel wool for scrubbing. Small pieces of steel filings left on the floor will rust and dis-color the terrazzo. Non-woven nylon or open-mesh fabric abrasive pads are suitable for scrubbing terrazzo floors.

1. According to the passage above, the BEST cleaning agent for terrazzo flooring is a(n)   1.____
   - A. soap cleaner
   - B. varnish preparation
   - C. neutral cleaner
   - D. alkaline solution

2. According to the passage above, terrazzo floors should NOT be scrubbed with   2.____
   - A. non-woven nylon abrasive pads
   - B. steel wool
   - C. open-mesh fabric abrasive pads
   - D. scouring powder

3. As used in the passage above, the word *discolor* means MOST NEARLY   3.____
   - A. crack   B. scratch   C. dissolve   D. stain

Questions 4-7.

DIRECTIONS: Questions 4 through 7 are to be answered in accordance with the information given in the following passage.

MOPPING FLOORS

When mopping hardened cement floors, either painted or unpainted, a soap and water mixture should be used. This should be made by dissolving half a cup of soft soap in a pail of hot water. It is not desirable, however, under any circumstances, to use a soap and water mixture on cement floors that are not hardened. For mopping this type of floor, it is recommended that the cleaning agent be made up of 2 ounces of laundry soda mixed in a pail of water.

Soaps are not generally used on hard tile floors because slippery films may build up on the floor. It is generally recommended that these floors be mopped using a pail of hot water in which has been mixed 2 ounces of washing powder for each gallon of water. The floors should then be rinsed thoroughly.

After the mopping is finished, proper care should be taken of the mop. This is done by first cleaning the mop in clear warm water. Then, it should be wrung out, after which the strands of the mop should be untangled. Finally, the mop should be hung by its handle to dry.

4. According to the above passage, you should NEVER use a soap and water mixture when mopping _____ floors.

    A. hardened cement
    B. painted
    C. unhardened cement
    D. unpainted

5. According to the above passage, using laundry soda mixed in a pail of water as a cleaning agent is recommended for

    A. all floors
    B. all floors except hard tile floors
    C. some cement floors
    D. linoleum floor coverings *only*

6. According to the above passage, the GENERALLY recommended mixture for mopping hard tile floors is _____ of hot water.

    A. 1/2 cup of soft soap for each gallon
    B. 1/2 cup of soft soap in a pail
    C. 2 ounces of washing powder in a pail
    D. 2 ounces of washing powder for each gallon

7. According to the above passage, the PROPER care of a mop after it is used includes

    A. cleaning it in clear cold water and hanging it by its handle to dry
    B. wringing it out, untangling and drying it
    C. untangling its strands before wringing it out
    D. untangling its strands while cleaning it in clear water

Questions 8-15.

DIRECTIONS: Questions 8 through 15 are to be answered ONLY in accordance with the following paragraph.

Many custodial foremen have discovered through experience that there are economies to be *realized* by using discretion when ordering items which are similar to each other. For example, it may be cheaper to order a *Sponge block, cellulose, WET SIZE: 6 in. x 4 3/4 in. x APPROXIMATELY 34 inches long* at $7.00 than it is to order separate *Sponges, cellulose, wet size: 2 in. x 4 in. x 6 in.* at 60¢. It does not pay to *over-order* on floor wax which may turn sour if not used soon enough. An average size college building cannot afford to have extra 30-inch floor brooms costing $19.75 each stored *on the shelf* for a couple of years or to let moths destroy the hair in such brooms if proper safeguards are not used.

8. According to the above passage, the items mentioned which are *similar* are 8.____

   A. floor brooms
   B. sponges
   C. floor waxes
   D. moths

9. As used in the above paragraph, the term *over-order* means to 9.____

   A. order again
   B. back order
   C. order too little
   D. order too much

10. Of the items for which prices are given in the above paragraph, the MOST expensive one is the 10.____

    A. 30-inch floor broom
    B. 6 in. x 4 3/4 in. x 34 in. sponge block
    C. 2 in. x 4 in. x 6 in. sponge
    D. floor wax

11. As used in the above paragraph, the word *realized* means MOST NEARLY 11.____

    A. obtained   B. lost   C. equalized   D. cheapened

12. According to the above paragraph, the one of the following which may be damaged by moths is the 12.____

    A. floor broom
    B. sponge
    C. cellulose
    D. wool cloth

13. As used in the above paragraph, the term *wet size* means 13.____

    A. the chemical treatment given to sponges
    B. the amount of water the sponge can hold
    C. that the sponges must be kept moist at all times
    D. that the measurements given were taken when the sponges were wet

14. As used in the above paragraph, the word *at* means 14.____

    A. near   B. arrived   C. each   D. new

15. As used in the above paragraph, the word *approximately* means 15.____

    A. exactly   B. about   C. economical   D. tan

Questions 16-17.

DIRECTIONS: Questions 16 and 17 are to be answered in accordance with the following paragraph.

Painting is done to preserve surfaces; and unless the surface is properly prepared, good preservation will not be possible. Apply paint only to clean dry surfaces. After a surface has been scaled, which means that all loose paint and rust are removed by chipping, scraping, and wire brushing, be sure all dust and dirt are completely removed.

16. According to the above paragraph, the MAIN purpose of painting a wall is to _____ the wall. 16._____

    A. clean
    B. waterproof
    C. protect
    D. remove dust from

17. According to the above paragraph, 17._____

    A. chipping, scraping, and wire brushing are the only methods permitted for cleaning surfaces
    B. painting is effective only when the surface is clean
    C. scaling refers only to the removal of rust
    D. paint may be applied on wet surfaces

Questions 18-21.

DIRECTIONS: Questions 18 through 21 are to be answered SOLELY on the basis of the following paragraph.

All cleaning agents and supplies should be kept in a central storeroom which should be kept locked and only the custodian, store-keeper, and foreman should have keys. Shelving should be provided for the smaller items while barrels containing scouring powder or other bulk material should be set on the floor or on special cradles. Each compartment in the shelves should be marked plainly and only the item indicated stored therein. Each barrel should also be marked plainly. It may also be desirable to keep special items such as electric lamps, flashlight batteries, etc. in a locked cabinet or separate room to which only the custodian and the night building foreman have keys.

18. According to the above paragraph, scouring powder 18._____

    A. should be kept on shelves
    B. comes in one-pound cans
    C. should be kept in a locked cabinet
    D. is a bulk material

19. According to the above paragraph, 19._____

    A. the storekeeper should not be entrusted with the safekeeping of light bulbs
    B. flashlight batteries should be stored in barrels
    C. the central storeroom should be kept locked
    D. only special items should be stored under lock and key

20. According to the above paragraph, 20._____

    A. each shelf compartment should contain at least four different items
    B. barrels must be stored in cradles
    C. all items stored should be in marked compartments
    D. crates of light bulbs should be stored in cradles

21. As used in the above paragraph, the word *cradle* means a 21._____

   A. dolly
   B. support
   C. doll's bed
   D. hand truck

Questions 22-25.

DIRECTIONS: Questions 22 through 25 are to be answered SOLELY on the basis of the following paragraph.

There are on the market many cleaning agents for which amazing claims are made. Chemical analysis shows that the majority of them are well-known chemicals slightly modified and packaged and sold under various trade names. For that reason, the agents which have been selected for your use are those whose cleaning properties are well-known and whose use can be standardized. It is obviously undesirable to offer too wide a selection as that would be confusing to the cleaner, but a sufficient number must be provided so that a satisfactory agent is available for each task.

22. According to the above paragraph, 22._____

   A. there are few cleaning agents on the market
   B. there are no really good cleaning agents on the market
   C. cleaning agents are sold under several different brand names
   D. all cleaning agents are the same

23. According to the above paragraph, 23._____

   A. all cleaning agents should be chemically analyzed before use
   B. the best cleaning agents are those for which no claims are made by the manufacturer
   C. different cleaning agents may be needed for different tasks
   D. all cleaning agents have been standardized by the federal government

24. As used in the above paragraph, the word *amazing* means 24._____

   A. illegal
   B. untrue
   C. astonishing
   D. specific

25. As used in the above paragraph, the word *modified* means 25._____

   A. changed   B. refined   C. labelled   D. diluted

KEY (CORRECT ANSWERS)

1.	C	11.	A
2.	B	12.	A
3.	D	13.	D
4.	C	14.	C
5.	C	15.	B
6.	D	16.	C
7.	B	17.	B
8.	B	18.	D
9.	D	19.	C
10.	A	20.	C

21. B
22. C
23. C
24. C
25. A

TEST 2

Questions 1-3.

DIRECTIONS: Questions 1 through 3 are to be answered in accordance with the following passage. Each question or incomplete statement is followed by several suggested answers or completions. Select the one that BEST answers the question or completes the statement. *PRINT THE LETTER OF THE CORRECT ANSWER IN THE SPACE AT THE RIGHT.*

    The method of cleaning which should generally be used is the space assignment method. Under this method, the buildings to be cleaned are divided into different sections. Within each section, each crew of Custodial Assistants is assigned to do one particular cleaning job. For example, within a section, one crew may be assigned to cleaning offices, another to scrubbing floors, a third to collecting trash, and so on. Other methods which may be used are the post assignment method and the gang cleaning method. Under the post assignment method, a Custodial Assistant is assigned to one area of a building and performs all cleaning jobs in that area. This method is seldom used except where buildings are so small and distant from each other that it is not economical to use the space assignment method. Under the gang cleaning method, a Custodial Foreman takes a number of Custodial Assistants through a section of the building. These Custodial Assistants work as a group and complete the various cleaning jobs as they go. This method is generally used only where the building contains very large open areas.

1. According to the passage above, under the space assignment method, each crew GENERALLY

    A. works as a group and does a variety of different cleaning jobs
    B. is assigned to one area and performs all cleaning jobs in that area
    C. does one particular cleaning job within a section of a building
    D. follows the Custodial Foreman through a building containing large, open areas

1.____

2. According to the passage above, the post assignment method is used MOSTLY where the buildings to be cleaned are _____ in size and situated _____.

    A. large; close together   B. small; close together
    C. large; far apart   D. small; far apart

2.____

3. As used in the passage above, the word *economical* means MOST NEARLY

    A. thrifty   B. agreed   C. unusual   D. wasteful

3.____

Questions 4-25.

DIRECTIONS: Each question consists of a statement. You are to indicate whether the statement is TRUE (T) or FALSE (F). *PRINT THE LETTER OF THE CORRECT ANSWER IN THE SPACE AT THE RIGHT.*

Questions 4-8.

DIRECTIONS: Questions 4 through 8 are to be answered in accordance with the information given in the following paragraph.

The removal of fine, loose dirt or dust from desks, chairs, filing cabinets, tables, and other furniture or office machines is called dusting. A yard of clean soft cloth, folded into a pad about nine inches square, is best for dusting. The cloth should be dry since oil or water on the cloth may streak the surface that is being dusted. When dusting a desk, care must be taken to put back in the same place any papers that were lifted or moved to one side. Thorough dusting of an office is important in order for the office to look neat and for the health of the people who work in that office.

4. The removal of fine, loose dirt or dust from furniture or office machines is called dusting. 4._____

5. A pad of cloth twelve inches square is best for dusting. 5._____

6. A dry cloth will streak the surface that is being dusted. 6._____

7. Papers that have been lifted or moved to one side when dusting a desk should be put back in the same place. 7._____

8. It is not important to dust an office thoroughly. 8._____

Questions 9-18.

DIRECTIONS: Questions 9 through 18 are to be answered in accordance with the information given in the following paragraphs.

WASHING OF WALLS

The washing of walls is important since wall-cleaning costs are an expensive item in the operating cost of building maintenance.

There is a right and a wrong way to wash walls. Streaks may be caused by water running down the dry wall below the place where one is working. This can be prevented by first wetting a section of the wall with water, starting at the bottom and working up before starting the actual washing operation with cleaning solution. Then, if the water runs down the wet wall, there will be almost no streaking. While washing a wall, the temperature should be reasonably low so that the water will not dry on the wall and cause streaks. Once the dirt on the wall is moistened, the wall must be kept wet until the dirt is removed. The washing of walls should be done with good sponges. One sponge should be for cleaning on the dirty wall and one for rinsing.

When working with the cleaning solution, start at the top of the wall and use a circular motion of the sponge and hand. Work across a given section first to the right and then to the left, and so on down to the base.

After the dirt has been removed, take clean, cool water and a clean sponge and go over the wall to be sure that it is perfectly clean and that no traces of the cleaning solution remain on the wall. Even clean water drying unevenly on a wall will cause slight streaks which become noticeable on the walls.

9. The amount of money spent to wash walls is a very small part in the expenses of running a building. 9._____

10. To prevent streaks when washing a wall, an employee should FIRST wet the wall, starting at the top and working down to the base of a wall. 10.____

11. If a wall is wet in the right way, there will be practically no streaks caused by water running down the wet wall. 11.____

12. If the walls are washed when the room is hot, streaks can be caused by water drying too quickly. 12.____

13. Once a dirty wall is made wet with water, it should be dried completely before the dirt is removed. 13.____

14. To wash walls properly, an employee should use at least two good sponges. 14.____

15. When washing with the cleaning solution, start at the bottom of the wall and work to the top, using a circular motion of the hand and sponge. 15.____

16. When washing with the cleaning solution, the CORRECT method is to work across each part of the wall going first to the left and ending on the right. 16.____

17. After the wall has been washed with the cleaning solution, it must be gone over again with clean water to remove any solution which is left on the wall. 17.____

18. When clean water is used to wash a wall, streaks will never appear, even if the wall dries unevenly. 18.____

Questions 19-25.

DIRECTIONS: Questions 19 through 25 are to be answered in accordance with the information given in the following passage.

CLEANING ELECTRIC LIGHT FIXTURES

A room may be dark not because there are not enough light fixtures but because the globes are dirty. As frequently as found necessary, and at least once a year, each globe on a light fixture should be taken down and carefully washed. It should be cleaned by using a solution of warm water to which has been added about two tablespoons full of washing soda for each 10 quarts of water. The globe must be thoroughly dried before it is put back or it is liable to crack from the heat of the lamp. At the time the globe is washed, the metal parts of the fixture should be wiped with a rag dampened in plain warm water. Most metal fixtures have been lacquered, and any cleaning solution would tend to destroy the lacquer. The electric light bulb should be unscrewed from the fixture and wiped with a slighly damp cloth. If it is burned out, it should be replaced at this time.

19. Dirty light globes will reduce the amount of light in a room. 19.____

20. Light globes should be cleaned only when the attendant replaces a burned out light bulb in a fixture. 20.____

21. To clean light globes, a solution of cold water and ordinary household ammonia should be used. 21.____

22. If a light globe is not completely dry when it is put back on a fixture after washing, the heat from the light bulb can break the globe. 22.____

23. The metal parts of a light fixture should be cleaned by using a dry rag to which has been added a few drops of a cleaning solution. 23.____

24. Most metal light fixtures have a coating of lacquer on them. 24.____

25. To clean a light bulb in a fixture, it should be unscrewed and wiped with a damp cloth. 25.____

KEY (CORRECT ANSWERS)

1.	C	11.	T
2.	D	12.	T
3.	A	13.	F
4.	T	14.	T
5.	F	15.	F
6.	F	16.	F
7.	T	17.	T
8.	F	18.	F
9.	F	19.	T
10.	F	20.	F
21.	F		
22.	T		
23.	F		
24.	T		
25.	T		

SUPERVISION STUDY GUIDE

Social science has developed information about groups and leadership in general and supervisor-employee relationships in particular. Since organizational effectiveness is closely linked to the ability of supervisors to direct the activities of employees, these findings are important to executives everywhere.

IS A SUPERVISOR A LEADER?

First-line supervisors are found in all large business and government organizations. They are the men at the base of an organizational hierarchy. Decisions made by the head of the organization reach them through a network of intermediate positions. They are frequently referred to as part of the management team, but their duties seldom seem to support this description.

A supervisor of clerks, tax collectors, meat inspectors, or securities analysts is not charged with budget preparation. He cannot hire or fire the employees in his own unit on his say-so. He does not administer programs which require great planning, coordinating, or decision making.

Then what is he? He is the man who is directly in charge of a group of employees doing productive work for a business or government agency. If the work requires the use of machines, the men he supervises operate them. If the work requires the writing of reports, the men he supervises write them. He is expected to maintain a productive flow of work without creating problems which higher levels of management must solve. But is he a leader?

To carry out a specific part of an agency's mission, management creates a unit, staffs it with a group of employees and designates a supervisor to take charge of them. Management directs what this unit shall do, from time to time changes directions, and often indicates what the group should not do. Management presumably creates status for the supervisor by giving him more pay, a title, and special privileges.

Management asks a supervisor to get his workers to attain organizational goals, including the desired quantity and quality of production. Supposedly, he has authority to enable him to achieve this objective. Management at least assumes that by establishing the status of the supervisor's position, it has created sufficient authority to enable him to achieve these goals—not his goals, nor necessarily the group's, but management's goals.

In addition, supervision includes writing reports, keeping records of membership in a higher-level administrative group, industrial engineering, safety engineering, editorial duties, housekeeping duties, etc. The supervisor as a member of an organizational network, must be responsible to the changing demands of the management above him. At the same time, he must be responsive to the demands of the work group of which he is a member. He is placed in the difficult position of communicating and implementing new decisions, changed programs and revised production quotas for his work group, although he may have had little part in developing them.

It follows, then, that supervision has a special characteristic: achievement of goals, previously set by management, through the efforts of others. It is in this feature of the supervisor's job that we find the role of a leader in the sense of the following definition: *A leader is that person who most effectively influences group activities toward goal setting and goal achievements.*

This definition is broad. It covers both leaders in groups that come together voluntarily and in those brought together through a work assignment in a factory, store, or government agency. In the natural group, the authority necessary to attain goals is determined by the group membership and is granted by them. In the working group, it is apparent that the establishment of a supervisory position creates a predisposition on the part of employees to accept the authority of the occupant of that position. We cannot, however, assume that mere occupation confers authority sufficient to assure the accomplishment of an organization's goals.

Supervision is different, then, from leadership. The supervisor is expected to fulfill the role of leader but without obtaining a grant of authority from the group he supervises. The supervisor is expected to influence the group in the achieving of goals but is often handicapped by having little influence on the organizational process by which goals are set. The supervisor, because he works in an organizational setting, has the burdens of additional organizational duties and restrictions and requirements arising out of the fact that his position is subordinate to a hierarchy of higher-level supervisors. These differences between leadership and supervision are reflected in our definition: *Supervision is basically a leadership role, in a formal organization, which has as its objective the effective influencing of other employees.*

Even though these differences between supervision and leadership exist, a significant finding of experimenters in this field is that supervisors must be leaders to be successful.

The problem is: How can a supervisor exercise leadership in an organizational setting? We might say that the supervisor is expected to be a natural leader in a situation which does not come about naturally. His situation becomes really difficult in an organization which is more eager to make its supervisors into followers rather than leaders.

LEADERSHIP: NATURAL AND ORGANIZATIONAL

Leadership, in its usual sense of *natural* leadership, and supervision are not the same. In some cases, leadership embraces broader powers and functions than supervision; in other cases, supervision embraces more than leadership. This is true both because of the organization and technical aspects of the supervisor's job and because of the relatively freer setting and inherent authority of the natural leader.

The natural leader usually has much more authority and influence than the supervisor. Group members not only follow his command but prefer it that way. The employee, however, can appeal the supervisor's commands to his union or to the supervisor's superior or to the personnel office. These intercessors represent restrictions on the supervisor's power to lead.

The natural leader can gain greater membership involvement in the group's objectives, and he can change the objectives of the group. The supervisor can attempt to gain employee support only for management's objectives; he cannot set other objectives. In these instances leadership is broader than supervision.

The natural leader must depend upon whatever skills are available when seeking to attain objectives. The supervisor is trained in the administrative skills necessary to achieve management's goals. If he does not possess the requisite skills, however, he can call upon management's technicians.

A natural leader can maintain his leadership, in certain groups, merely by satisfying members' need for group affiliation. The supervisor must maintain his leadership by directing and organizing his group to achieve specific organizational goals set for him and his group by management. He must have a technical competence and a kind of coordinating ability which is not needed by many natural leaders.

A natural leader is responsible only to his group which grants him authority. The supervisor is responsible to management, which employs him, and also to the work group of which he is a member. The supervisor has the exceedingly difficult job of reconciling the demands of two groups frequently in conflict. He is often placed in the untenable position of trying to play two antagonistic roles. In the above instance, supervision is broader than leadership.

ORGANIZATIONAL INFLUENCES ON LEADERSHIP

The supervisor is both a product and a prisoner of the organization wherein we find him. The organization which creates the supervisor's position also obstructs, restricts, and channelizes the exercise of his duties. These influences extend beyond prescribed functional relationships to specific supervisory behavior. For example, even in a face-to-face situation involving one of his subordinates, the supervisor's actions are controlled to a great extent by his organization. His behavior must conform to the organization policy on human relations, rules which dictate personnel procedures, specific prohibitions governing conduct, the attitudes of his own superior, etc. He is not a free agent operating within the limits of his work group. His freedom of action is much more circumscribed than is generally admitted. The organizational influences which limit his leadership actions can be classified as structure, prescriptions, and proscriptions.

The organizational structure places each supervisor's position in context with other designated positions. It determines the relationships between his position and specific positions which impinge on his. The structure of the organization designates a certain position to which he looks for orders and information about his work. It gives a particular status to his position within a pattern of statuses from which he perceives that (1) certain positions are on a par, organizationally, with his, (2) other positions are subordinate, and (3) still others are superior.

The organizational structure determines those positions to which he should look for advice and assistance, and those positions to which he should give advice and assistance.

For instance, the organizational structure has predetermined that the supervisor of a clerical processing unit shall report to a supervisory position in a higher echelon. He shall have certain relationships with the supervisors of the work units which transmit work to and receive work from his unit. He shall discuss changes and clarification of procedures with certain staff units, such as organization and methods, cost accounting, and personnel. He shall consult supervisors of units which provide or receive special work assignments.

The organizational structure, however, establishes patterns other than those of the relationships of positions. These are the patterns of responsibility, authority, and expectations.

The supervisor is responsible for certain activities or results; he is presumably invested with the authority to achieve these. His set of authority and responsibility is interwoven with other sets to the end that all goals and functions of the organization are parceled out in small, manageable lots. This, of course, establishes a series of expectations: a single supervisor can perform his particular set of duties only upon the assumption that preceding or contiguous sets of duties have been, or are being carried out. At the same time, he is aware of the expectations of others that he will fulfill his functional role.

The structure of an organization establishes relationships between specified positions and specific expectations for these positions. The fact that these relationships and expectations are established is one thing; whether or not they are met is another.

PRESCRIPTIONS AND PROSCRIPTIONS

But let us return to the organizational influences which act to restrict the supervisor's exercise of leadership. These are the prescriptions and proscriptions generally in effect in all organizations, and those peculiar to a single organization. In brief these are the *thou shalt's* and the *thou shalt not's*.

Organizations not only prescribe certain duties for individual supervisory positions, they also prescribe specific methods and means of carrying out these duties and maintaining management-employee relations. These include rules, regulations, policy, and tradition. It does no good for the supervisor to say, *This seems to be the best way to handle such-and-such,* if the organization has established a routine for dealing with problems. For good or bad, there are rules that state that firings shall be executed in such a manner, accompanied by a certain notification; that training shall be conducted, and in this manner. Proscriptions are merely negative prescriptions; you may not discriminate against any employee because of politics or race; you shall not suspend any employee without following certain procedures and obtaining certain approvals.

Most of these prohibitions and rules apply to the area of interpersonal relations, precisely the area which is now arousing most interest on the part of administrators and managers. We have become concerned about the contrast between formally prescribed relationships and interpersonal relationships, and this brings us to the often discussed informal organization.

FORMAL AND INFORMAL ORGANIZATIONS

As we well know, the functions and activities of any organization are broken down into individual units of work called positions. Administrators must establish a pattern which will link these positions to each other and relate them to a system of authority and responsibility. Man-to-man are spelled out as plainly as possible for all to understand. Managers, then, build an official structure which we call the formal organization.

In these same organizations, employees react individually and in groups to institutionally determined roles. John, a worker, rides in the same carpool as Joe, a foreman. An unplanned communication develops. Harry, a machinist knows more about high-speed machining than his foreman or anyone else in his shop. An unofficial tool boss comes into being. Mary, who fought with Jane, is promoted over her. Jane now gives Mary's directions. A planned relationship fails to develop. The employees have built a structure which we call the informal organization.

Formal organization is a system of management-prescribed relations between positions in an organization.

Informal organization is a network of unofficial relations between people in an organization.

These definitions might lead us to the absurd conclusion that positions carry out formal activities and that employe4es spend their time in unofficial activities. We must recognize that organizational activities are in all cases carried out by people. The formal structure provides a needed framework within which interpersonal relations occur. What we call informal organization is the complex of normal, natural relations among employees. These personal relationships may be negative or positive. That is, they may impede or aid the achievement of organizational goals. For example, friendship between two supervisors greatly increases the probability of good cooperation and coordination between their sections. On the other hand, *buck passing* nullifies the formal structure by failure to meet a prescribed and expected responsibility.

It is improbable that an ideal organization exists where all activities are carried out in strict conformity to a formally prescribed pattern of functional roles. Informal organization arises because of the incompleteness and ambiguities in the network of formally prescribed relationships, or in response to the needs or inadequacies of supervisors or managers who hold prescribed functional roles in an organization. Many of these relationships are not prescribed by the organizational pattern; many cannot be prescribed; many should not be prescribed.

Management faces the problem of keeping the informal organization in harmony with the mission of the agency. One way to do this is to make sure that all employees have a clear understanding of and are sympathetic with that mission. The issuance of organizational charts, procedural manuals, and functional descriptions of the work to be done by divisions and sections helps communicate management's plans and goals. Issuances alone, of course, cannot do the whole job. They should be accompanied by oral discussion and explanation. Management must ensure that there is mutual understanding and acceptance of charts and procedures. More important is that management acquaint itself with the attitudes, activities, and peculiar brands of logic which govern the informal organization. Only through this type of knowledge can they and supervisors keep informal goals consistent with the agency mission.

SUPERVISION STATUS AND FUNCTIONAL ROLE

A well-established supervisor is respected by the employees who work with him. They defer to his wishes. It is clear that a superior-subordinate relationship has been established. That is, status of the supervisor has been established in relation to other employees of the same work group. This same supervisor gains the respect of employees when he behaves in as certain manner. He will be expected, generally, to follow the customs of the group in such matters as dress, recreation, and manner of speaking. The group has a set of expectations as to his behavior. His position is a functional role which carries with it a collection of rights and obligations.

The position of supervisor usually has a status distinct from the individual who occupies it: it is much like a position description which exists whether or not there is an incumbent. The status of a supervisory position is valued higher than that of an employee position both because of the functional role of leadership which is assigned to it and because of the status symbols of titles, rights, and privileges which go with it.

Social ranking, or status, is not simple because it involves both the position and the man. An individual may be ranked higher than others because of his education, social background, perceived leadership ability, or conformity to group customs and ideals. If such a man is ranked higher by the members of a work group than their supervisor, the supervisor's effectiveness may be seriously undermined.

If the organization does not build and reinforce a supervisor's status, his position can be undermined in a different way. This will happen when managers go around rather than through the supervisor or designate him as a straw boss, acting boss, or otherwise not a real boss.

Let us clarify this last point. A role, and corresponding status, establishes a set of expectations. Employees expect their supervisor to do certain things and to act in certain ways. They are prepared to respond to that expected behavior. When the supervisor's behavior does not conform to their expectations, they are surprised, confused, and ill-at-ease. It becomes necessary for them to resolve their confusion, if they can. They might do this by turning to one of their own members for leadership. If the confusion continues, or their attempted solutions are not satisfactory, they will probably become a poorly motivated, non-cohesive group which cannot function very well.

COMMUNICATION AND THE SUPERVISOR

In a recent survey, railroad workers reported that they rarely look to their supervisor for information about the company. This is startling, at least to us, because we ordinarily think of the supervisor as the link between management and worker. We expect the supervisor to be the prime source of information about the company. Actually, the railroad workers listed the supervisor next to last in the o5rder of their sources of information. Most surprising of all, the supervisors, themselves, stated that rumor and unofficial contacts were their principal sources of information. Here we see one of the reasons why supervisors may not be as effective as management desires.

The supervisor is not only being bypassed by his work group, he is being ignored, and his position weakened, by the very organization which is holding him responsible for the activities of his workers. If he is management's representative to the employee, then management has an obligation to keep him informed of its activities. This is necessary if he is to carry out his functions efficiently and maintain his leadership in the work group. The supervisor is expected to be a source of information; when he is not, his status is not clear, and employees are dissatisfied because he has not lived up to expectations.

By providing information to the supervisor to pass along to employees, we can strengthen his position as leader of the group, and increase satisfaction and cohesion within the group. Because he has more information than the other members, receives information sooner, and passes it along at the proper times, members turn to him as a source and also provide him with information in the hope of receiving some in return. From this, we can see an increase in group cohesiveness because:

- Employees are bound closer to their supervisor because he is *in the know*.
- There is less need to go outside the group for answers
- Employees will more quickly turn to the supervisor for enlightenment

The fact that he has the answers will also enhance the supervisor's standing in the eyes of his men. This increased status will serve to bolster his authority and control of the group and will probably result in improved morale and productivity.

The foregoing, of course, does not mean that all management information should be given out. There are obviously certain policy determinations and discussions which need not or cannot be transmitted to all supervisors. However, the supervisor must be kept as fully informed as possible so that he can answer questions when asked and can allay needless fears and anxieties. Further, the supervisor has the responsibility of encouraging employee questions and submissions of information. He must be able to present information to employees so that it is clearly understood and accepted. His attitude and manner should make it clear that he believes in what he is saying, that the information is necessary or desirable to the group, and that he is prepared to act on the basis of the information.

SUPERVISION AND JOB PERFORMANCE

The productivity of work groups is a product; employees' efforts are multiplied by the supervision they receive. Many investigators have analyzed this relationship and have discovered elements of supervision which differentiate high and low production groups. These researchers have identified certain types of supervisory practices which they classify as *employee-centered* and other types which they classify as *production centered*.

The difference between these two kinds of supervision lies not in specific practices but in the approach or orientation to supervision. The employee-centered supervisor directs most of his efforts toward increasing employee motivation. He is concerned more with realizing the potential energy of persons than with administrative and technological methods of increasing efficiency and productivity. He is the man who finds ways of causing employees to want to work harder with the same tools. These supervisors emphasize the personal relations between their employees and themselves.

Now, obviously, these pictures are overdrawn. No one supervisor has all the virtues of the ideal type of employee-centered supervisor. And, fortunately, no one supervisor has all the bad traits found in many production-centered supervisors. We should remember that the various practices that researchers have fond which distinguish these two kinds of supervision represent the many practices and methods of supervisors of all gradations between these extremes. We should be careful, too, of the implications of the labels attached to the two types. For instance, being production-centered is not necessarily bad, since the principal responsibility of any supervisor is maintaining the production level that is expected of his work group. Being employee-centered may not necessarily be good, if the only result is a happy, chuckling crew of loafers. To return to the researchers' findings, employee-centered supervisors:

- Recommend promotions, transfers, pay increases
- Inform men about what is happening in the company
- Keep men posted on how well they are doing
- Hear complaints and grievances sympathetically
- Speak up for subordinates

Production-centered supervisors, on the other hand, don't do those things. They check on employees more frequently, give more detailed and frequent instructions, don't give reasons for changes, and are more punitive when mistakes are made. Employee-centered supervisors were reported to contribute to high morale and high production, whereas production-centered supervision was associated with lower morale and less production.

More recent findings, however, show that the relationship between supervision and productivity is not this simple. Investigators now report that high production is more frequently associated with supervisory practices which combine employee-centered behavior with concern for production. (This concern is not the same, however, as anxiety about production, which is the hallmark of our production-centered supervisor.) Let us examine these apparently contradictory findings and the premises from which they are derived.

SUPERVISION AND MORALE

Why do supervisory activities cause high or low production? As the name implies, the activities of the employee-centered supervisor tend to relate him more closely and satisfactorily to his workers. The production-centered supervisor's practices tend to separate him from his group and to foster antagonism. An analysis of this difference may answer our question.

Earlier, we pointed out that the supervisor is a type of leader and that leadership is intimately related to the group in which it occurs We discover, now, that an employee-centered supervisor's primary activities are concerned with both his leadership and his group membership. Such a supervisor is a member of a group and occupies a leadership role in that group.

These facts are sometimes obscured when we speak of the supervisor as management's representative, or as the organizational link between management and the employee, or as the end of the chain of command. If we really want to understand what it is we expect of the supervisor, we must remember that he is the designated leader of a group of employees to whom he is bound by interaction and interdependence.

Most of his actions are aimed, consciously or unconsciously, at strengthening membership ties in the group. This includes both making members more conscious that he is a member of their group) and causing members to identify themselves more closely with the group. These ends are accomplished by:

- making the group more attractive to the worker: they find satisfaction of their needs for recognition, friendship, enjoyable work, etc.;
- maintaining open communication: employees can express their views and obtain information about the organization
- giving assistance: members can seek advice on personal problems as well as their work; and
- acting as a buffer between the group and management: he speaks up for his men and explains the reasons for management's decisions.

Such actions both strengthen group cohesiveness and solidarity and affirm the supervisor's leadership position in the group.

DEFINING MORALE

This brings us back to a point mentioned earlier. We had said that employee-centered supervisors contribute to high morale as well as to high production. But how can we explain units which have low morale and high productivity, or vice versa? Usually production and morale are considered separately, partly because they are measured against different criteria and partly because, in some instances, they seem to be independent of each other.

Some of this difficulty may stem from confusion over definitions of morale. Morale has been defined as, or measured by, absences from work, satisfaction with job or company, dissension among members of work groups, productivity, apathy or lack of interest, readiness to help others, and a general aura of happiness as rated by observers. Some of these criteria of morale are not subject to the influence of the supervisor, and some of them are not clearly related to productivity. Definitions like these invite findings of low morale coupled with high production.

Both productivity and morale can be influenced by environmental factors not under the control of group members or supervisors. Such things as plant layout, organizational structure and goals, lighting, ventilation, communications, and management planning may have an adverse or desirable effect.

We might resolve the dilemma by defining morale on the basis of our understanding of the supervisor as leader of a group; morale is the degree of satisfaction of group members with their leadership. In this light, the supervisor's employee-centered activities bear a clear relation to morale. His efforts to increase employee identification with the group and to strengthen his leadership lead to greater satisfaction with that leadership. By increasing group cohesiveness and by demonstrating that his influence and power can aid the group, he is able to enhance his leadership status and afford satisfaction to the group.

SUPERVISION, PRODUCTION, AND MORALE

There are factors within the organization itself which determine whether increased production is possible:

- Are production goals expressed in terms understandable to employees and are they realistic?
- Do supervisors responsible for production respect the agency mission and production goals?
- If employees do not know how to do the job well, does management provide a trainer—often the supervisor—who can teach efficient work methods?

There are other factors within the work group which determine whether increased production will be attained:

- Is leadership present which can bring about the desired level of production?
- Are production goals accepted by employees as reasonable and attainable?
- If group effort is involved, are members able to coordinate their efforts?

Research findings confirm the view that an employee-centered supervisor can achieve higher morale than a production-centered supervisor. Managers may well ask what is the relationship between this and production.

Supervision is production-oriented to the extent that it focuses attention on achieving organizational goals, and plans and devises methods for attaining them; it is employee-centered to the extent that it focuses attention on employee attitudes toward those goals, and plans and works toward maintenance of employee satisfaction.

High productivity and low morale result when a supervisor plans and organizes work efficiently but cannot achieve high membership satisfaction. Low production and high morale result when a supervisor, though keeping members satisfied with his leadership, either has not gained acceptance of organizational goals or does not have the technical competence to achieve them.

The relationship between supervision, morale, and productivity is an interdependent one, with the supervisor playing an integral role due to his ability to influence productivity and morale independently of each other.

A supervisor who can plan his work well has good technical knowledge, and who can install better production methods can raise production without necessarily increasing group satisfaction. On the other hand, a supervisor who can motivate his employees and keep them satisfied with his leadership can gain high production in spite of technical difficulties and environmental obstacles.

CLIMATE AND SUPERVISION

Climate, the intangible environment of an organization made up of attitudes, beliefs, and traditions, plays a large part in morale, productivity, and supervision. Usually when we speak of climate and its relationship to morale and productivity, we talk about the merits of *democratic* versus *authoritarian* climate. Employees seem to produce more and have higher morale in a democratic climate, whereas in an authoritarian climate, the reverse seems to be true or so the researchers tell us. We would do well to determine what these terms mean to supervision.

Perhaps most of our difficulty in understanding and applying these concepts comes from our emotional reactions to the words themselves. For example, authoritarian climate is usually painted as the very blackest kind of dictatorship. This is not surprising, because we are usually expected to believe that it is invariably bad. Conversely, democratic climate is drawn to make the driven snow look impure by comparison.

Now these descriptions are most probably true when we talk about our political processes, or town meetings, or freedom of speech. However, the same labels have been used by social scientists in other contexts and have also been applied to government and business organizations, without it, it seems, any recognition that the meanings and their social values may have changed somewhat

For example, these labels were used in experiments conducted in an informal classroom setting using 11-year-old boys as subjects. The descriptive labels applied to the climate of the setting as well as the type of leadership practiced. When these labels were transferred to a management setting, it seems that many presumed that they principally meant the king of leadership rather than climate. We can see that there is a great difference between the experimental and management settings and that leadership practices for one might be inappropriate for the other.

It is doubtful that formal work organizations can be anything but authoritarian, in that goals are set by management and a hierarchy exists through which decisions and orders from the top are transmitted downward. Organizations are authoritarian by structure and need; direction and control are placed in the hands of a few in order to gain fast and efficient decision making. Now this does not mean to describe a dictatorship. It is merely the recognition of the fact that direction of organizational affairs comes from above. It should be noted that leadership in some natural groups is, in this sense, authoritarian.

Granting that formal organizations have this kind of authoritarian leadership, can there be a democratic climate? Certainly there can be, but we would want to define and delimit this term. A more realistic meaning of democratic climate in organizations is the use of permissive and participatory methods in management-employee relations. That is, a mutual exchange of information and explanation with the granting of individual freedom within certain restricted and defined limits. However, it is not our purpose to debate the merits of authoritarianism versus democracy. We recognize that within the small work group there is a need for freedom from constraint and an increase in participation in order to achieve organizational goals within the framework of the organizational movement.

Another aspect of climate is best expressed by this familiar, and true, saying: actions speak louder than words. Of particular concern to us is this effect of management climate on the behavior of supervisors, particularly in employee-centered activities.

There have been reports of disappointment with efforts to make supervisors ore employee-centered. Managers state that, since research has shown ways of improving human relations, supervisors should begin to practice these methods. Usually a training course in human relations is established; and supervisors are given this training. Managers then sit back and wait for the expected improvements, only to find that there are none.

If we wish to produce changes in the supervisor's behavior, the climate must be made appropriate and rewarding to the changed behavior. This means that top-level attitudes and behavior cannot deny or contradict the change we are attempting to effect. Basic changes in organizational behavior cannot be made with any permanence, unless we provide an environment that is receptive to the changes and rewards those persons who do change.

IMPROVING SUPERVISION

Anyone who has read this far might expect to find *A Dozen Rules for Dealing With Employees* or *29 Steps to Supervisory Success*. We will not provide such a list.

Simple rules suffer from their simplicity. They ignore the complexities of human behavior. Reliance upon rules may cause supervisors to concentrate on superficial aspects of their relations with employees. It may preclude genuine understanding.

The supervisor who relies on a list of rules tends to think of people in mechanistic terms. In a certain situation, he uses *Rule No. 3*. Employees are not treated as thinking and feeling persons, but rather as figures in a formula: Rule 3 applied to employee X = Production.

Employees usually recognize mechanical manipulation and become dissatisfied and resentful. They lose faith in, and respect for, their supervisor, and this may be reflected in lower morale and productivity.

We do not mean that supervisors must become social science experts if they wish to improve. Reports of current research indicate that there are two major parts of their job which can be strengthened through self-improvement: (1) Work planning, including technical skills, and (2) motivation of employees.

The most effective supervisors combine excellence in the administrative and technical aspects of their work with friendly and considerate personal relations with their employees.

CRITICAL PERSONAL RELATIONS

Later in this chapter we shall talk about administrative aspects of supervision, but first let us comment on *friendly and considerate personal relations*. We have discussed this subject throughout the preceding chapters, but we want to review some of the critical supervisory influences on personal relations.

Closeness of Supervision: The closeness of supervision has an important effect on productivity and morale. Mann and Dent found that supervisors of low-producing units supervise very closely, while high-producing supervisors exercise only general supervision. It was found that the low-producing supervisors:

- check on employees more frequently
- give more detailed and frequent instructions
- limit employee's freedom to do job in own way

Workers who felt less closely supervised reported that they were better satisfied with their jobs and the company. We should note that the manner or attitude of the supervisor has an important bearing on whether employees perceive supervision as being close or general.

These findings are another way of saying that supervision does not mean standing over the employee and telling him what to do and when and how to do it. The more effective supervisor tells his employees what is required, giving general instructions.

COMMUNICATION

Supervisors of high-production units consider communication as one of the most important aspects of their job. Effective communication is used by these supervisors to achieve better interpersonal relations and improved employee motivation. Low-production supervisors do not rate communications as highly important.

High-producing supervisors find that an important aid to more effective communication is listening. They are ready to listen to both personal problems or interests and questions about the work. This does not mean that they are *nosey* or meddle in their employees' personal lives, but rather that they show a willingness to listen, and do listen, if their employees wish to discuss problems.

These supervisors inform employees about forthcoming changes in work; they discuss agency policy with employees; and they make sure that each employee knows how well he is doing. What these supervisors do is use two-way communication effectively. Unless the supervisor freely imparts information, he will not receive information in return.

Attitudes and perception are frequently affected by communication or the lack of it. Research surveys reveal that many supervisors are not aware of their employees' attitudes, nor do they know what personal reactions their supervision arouses. Through frank discussion with employees, they have been surprised to discover employee beliefs about which they were ignorant. Discussion sometimes reveals that the supervisor and his employees have totally different impressions about the same event. The supervisor should be constantly on the alert for misconceptions about his words and deeds. He must remember that, although his actions are perfectly clear to himself, they may be, and frequently are, viewed differently by employees.

Failure to communicate information results in misconceptions and false assumptions. What you say and how you say it will strongly affect your employees' attitudes and perceptions. By giving them available information, you can prevent misconceptions; by discussion, you may be able to change attitudes; by questioning, you can discover what the perceptions and assumptions really are. And it need hardly be added that actions should conform very closely to words.

If we were to attempt to reduce the above discussion on communication to rules, we would have a long list which would be based on one cardinal principle: Don't make assumptions!

- Don't assume that your employees know; tell them.
- Don't assume that you know how they feel; find out.
- Don't assume that they understand; clarify.

20 SUPERVISORY HINTS

1. Avoid inconsistency.
2. Always give employees a chance to explain their action before taking disciplinary action. Don't allow too much time for a "cooling off" period before disciplining an employee.
3. Be specific in your criticisms.
4. Delegate responsibility wisely.
5. Do not argue or lose your temper, and avoid being impatient.
6. Promote mutual respect and be fair, impartial, and open-minded.
7. Keep in mind that asking for employees' advice and input can be helpful in decision making.
8. If you make promises, keep them.
9. Always keep the feelings, abilities, dignity and motives of your staff in mind.
10. Remain loyal to your employees' interests.
11. Never criticize employees in front of others, or treat employees like children.
12. Admit mistakes. Don't place blame on your employees, or make excuses.
13. Be reasonable in your expectations, give complete instructions, and establish well-planned goals.
14. Be knowledgeable about office details and procedures, but avoid becoming bogged down in details.
15. Avoid supervising too closely or too loosely. Employees should also view you as an approachable supervisor.
16. Remember that employees' personal problems may affect job performance, but become involved only when appropriate.
17. Work to develop workers, and to instill a feeling of cooperation while working toward mutual goals.
18. Do not overpraise or underpraise, be properly appreciative.
19. Never ask an employee to discipline someone for you.
20. A complaint, even if unjustified, should be taken seriously.

NOTES

www.ingramcontent.com/pod-product-compliance
Lightning Source LLC
Chambersburg PA
CBHW081822300426
44116CB00014B/2458